MODERN LEGAL STUDIES

Advertising, Culture and the Law:
Beyond Lies, Ignorance and Manipulation

IAIN RAMSAY
Professor of Law, Osgoode Hall Law School
York University, Canada

London
Sweet & Maxwell
1996

Published in 1996
by Sweet & Maxwell Limited of
100 Avenue Road, Swiss Cottage, London, NW3 3PF
Typeset by Selwood Systems, Midsomer Norton
Printed in England by Clays Ltd, St Ives plc

No natural forests were destroyed to make this product;
only farmed timber was used and then replanted.
A CIP catalogue record for this book is available
from the British Library.

ISBN 0421 52650 5

© Iain Ramsay 1996

For Toni

Preface

This book grew out of research which I began in the late 1980s into the regulation of advertising to children. It soon became clear that this research raised broader questions about the power of advertising in society and legal assumptions concerning the impact and effects of advertising. In addition, there was an enormous growth of interest in consumer culture associated with the rise of cultural studies. This book is an attempt therefore to investigate legal and cultural ideas about the power of advertising, situating them in the context of legal doctrines and against the background of theories concerning the changing nature of consumer capitalism.

The book draws on a broad variety of sources, such as feminism, cultural studies, law and economics and critical race theory, and is necessarily eclectic in its selection of these sources. The purpose throughout is to raise questions about existing legal assumptions and suggest new avenues for the law. It is worthwhile emphasising here the perspective of the book. The dominant ideas about advertising which I discuss in the text are primarily North American. While these ideas may not yet have colonised all societies, they are increasingly having an international impact. They are tied to the spread of consumerism throughout many parts of the world and deserve close scrutiny.

I would like to acknowledge the following debts. Reuben Hasson, Toni Williams and Thomas Wilhelmsson provided valuable comments on the text. I am grateful to the Canadian Social Sciences and Humanities Research Council for the original grant to study the regulation of advertising to children. Didi Herman, now a senior lecturer at Keele University, contributed valuable research assistance on the original study of advertising to children. Finally, Sweet and Maxwell provided excellent editorial assistance.

Iain Ramsay
Toronto, September 1996.

Contents

Table of Cases

American Cases

Canadian Cases

British and European Cases

Table of Statutes

Chapter 1

Introduction

"[E]verything in our social life—from economic value and state power to practices and to the very structure of the psyche itself—can be said to have become 'cultural' in some original and yet untheorized sense".

(Frederick Jameson, *Post-Modernism or the Cultural Logic of Late Capitalism* (1991), p. 48).

"We live of course in a world not only of commodities but also of representation, and representations—their production, circulation, history and interpretation—are the very element of culture."

(Edward Said, *Culture and Imperialism* (1993), p. 56).

There has been an avalanche of books and articles in recent years analysing the nature and significance of the contemporary social and cultural aspects of the consumer society.[1] A major theme in this literature is that although capitalism has become a dominant social formation, it is consumption, rather than production, which provides the system with its legitimacy and gives meaning to individuals' lives. Consumption has become a site of economic, social, cultural and political relations which can no longer be viewed as the merely epiphenomenal consequence of particular production relations.

This new phase in the development of capitalism underlies much discussion of the post-modern or consumer society.[2] Consumerism seems to provide an

---

[1] See below, App. 1: *Further Reading* for references to some of this literature.

[2] Jameson describes post-modernism as bearing "a strong family resemblance to all those more ambitious sociological generalizations which ... bring us the news of the arrival and inauguration of a whole new type of society, most famously baptized 'postindustrial society' (Daniel Bell) but often also designated consumer society, media society, information society ... Such theories have the obvious ideological mission of demonstrating, to their own relief, that the new social formation in question no longer obeys the laws

important link in arguments concerning the supposed convergence of disparate
societies whether one is discussing developments in Eastern Europe or the
newly emerging economies of Latin America or South East Asia. Some writers
appeal to the image of the citizen as consumer as empowering and democratic;
others associate consumerism with dystopian visions of a passive citizenry in a
society dominated by commercial interests where politics and the public sphere
are infected by the values of a promotional culture. Citizenship has been traded
for consumerism.

Disagreements over the values associated with the consumer society recognise
that consumption is more than a process of material accumulation. Goods and
services are purchased not just for material use but as part of an idealistic
practice. Individuals may associate goods with "imaginative pleasure seeking
to which the product lends itself"[3] or as part of a lifestyle. The objects may be
part of a continuing attempt to construct identities around the signs associated
with the objects or the meaning associated with the particular experience of
consumption. The American writer Don de Lillo comments that "[t]o consume
in America is not to buy; it is to dream."[4]

The commercial media with its pervasive advertising images of affluence
and success is a central institution of consumer capitalism. The reach of the
media ensures that desires for identity through consumption permeate society
at all levels of income. They do not disappear simply because of economic
recessions. The cultural idea of consumerism is deeply entwined with the
economic system so that in the consumer society material deprivation may go
hand-in-hand with a strong sense of cultural exclusion. Developing this theme,
Cornel West argues that the contemporary "culture of consumption" has a
particularly alienating and destructive impact on the lives of the urban, black
poor in the USA.[5] At the same time the ubiquity of the commercial media
throughout the world ensures that the idea, if not the practice, of consumerism
becomes a global presence.

Advertising plays a central role in consumer capitalism, in extending markets,
and creating images of social relations of consumption. It is not surprising,

---

of classical capitalism, namely the primacy of industrial production and the omnipresence
of class struggle". F. Jameson, *Post-Modernism or, The Cultural Logic of Late Capitalism* (1991),
p. 3.
[3] C. Campbell, *The Romantic Ethic and the Spirit of Modern Consumerism* (1987), p. 189, quoted
in K. Thompson, *Key Quotations in Sociology* (1996), p. 27.
[4] D. de Lillo, *Americana* (1989), pp. 431–432.
[5] C. West, *Race Matters* (1993), p. 5 and see generally R. Austin, "A Nation of Thieves":
Securing Black People's Right to Shop and Sell in White America" (1994) Utah L.R.
147. For analysis of the intense marketing of black neighbourhoods through billboard
campaigns by cigarette companies, see R. Pollay, J. S. Lee, and D. Carter-Whitney
"Separate, But Not Equal: Racial Segmentation in Advertising" (1992) 21: 1 *Journal of
Advertising* 45.

therefore, that many students of contemporary consumer culture have focused on advertising in their discussions and critiques of consumer culture.[6] Social movements, such as feminism and minority rights advocacy, have viewed cultural images and representations in the media and commercial advertising as an important site for social change, appealing to the legal regulation of images as a method of social change.[7] Advertising images may represent, within this critique, unfair cultural practices.[8]

Very little of this rich literature has influenced legal thinking about advertising in consumer markets, or legal theories as to the power of advertising over consumer taste and behaviour. This seems curious since the law is, in many countries, involved in important practical decisions on such topics as advertising to children, the regulation of tobacco advertising, the portrayal of women and minorities, the "selling" of the environment, and the protection of national cultures. A brief review of legal debates in this area indicates that the issues are often cultural in nature: they raise questions about the commodification of aspects of social life, such as the commercialisation of childhood, or the politics of the policing of images and representations of social groups.

This book is an exploration of the power of advertising, as it is understood in legal and cultural discourse. A central theme is the contribution of advertising to cultural domination and the role of law and legal discourse in addressing the cultural power of advertising images. I argue that assumptions about consumer behaviour and standard conceptions of the power of advertising in legal and public policy discourse, are limited in addressing many of the cultural aspects of advertising.

There are three main narratives in advertising law: truth in advertising;

---

[6] For example, Stuart Ewen's history of the growth of consumer capitalism in the USA focuses on advertising. See S. Ewen, *Captains of Consciousness: Advertising and the Roots of the Consumer Culture* (1976). Advertising is also an important part of Susan Bordo's feminist analysis of the oppression of women in consumer capitalism. See S. Bordo, *Unbearable Weight: Feminism, Western Culture and the Body* (1993).

[7] See, *e.g.* in relation to sex role stereotyping, A. Courtney and T. Whipple, *Sex Stereotyping in Advertising* (1983); L. Trimble, "Coming Soon to A Station Near You? The CRTC Policy on Sex-Role Stereotyping" in *Seeing Ourselves: Media Power and Policy in Canada* (H. Holmes and D. Taras, ed. 1992). On the damaging impact of advertising stereotypes on women see N. Wolf, *The Beauty Myth: How Images of Beauty are used against women* (1992). See also E. Goffman, *Gender advertisements* (1979). For a discussion of the role of images as part of housing discrimination in the USA and a proposal for image equality see R. L. Robinson, "The Racial Limits of the Fair Housing Act: The Intersection of Dominant White Images, The Violence of Neighborhood Purity, and the Master Narrative of Black Inferiority" (1995) 37 *Wm. & Mary L.* 69. See also below, Chap. 4, at pp. 118–138.

[8] In describing the anti-pornography movement to regulate pornographic images (which use similar techniques to advertising) Sullivan notes that "[P]ornography operate[s] as a kind of cultural unfair trade practice". K. Sullivan, "Free Speech and unfree Markets" (1995) 42 *U.C.L.A. L. Rev.* 949 at 956.

advertising as information; advertising as preference manipulation. Advertising as information is currently the dominant narrative in many countries, having almost attained the level of common sense. Its influence is apparent in the decisions of courts and administrative agencies in North America and Europe. Advertising is conceived as information and regulation is regarded as a method of market intervention to ensure an adequate flow of information to consumers. The dominance of this information narrative is attributable partly to the influence of neo-classical economics, and the current ideology of "the market" as an empowering and liberating force. The rise of the argument that advertising should be provided with constitutional protection under the doctrine of commercial speech in the USA and Canada has also underlined the importance of advertising as information, emphasising "listeners' rights" to information.[9] This doctrine has also been of great material benefit to corporate advertisers in their attacks on regulation of advertising in North America and Europe.

Within this dominant narrative the primary purpose of regulation, either by a court or regulator, is not to substitute its preferences for those of the consumer but to ensure the protection of the reasonable or rational consumer against information failures. While the law might recognise that advertising might manipulate particularly vulnerable audiences, this is regarded as an exception to the norm. Proposals which appear to go beyond these boundaries, for example, regulation of advertising based on concerns about exploitation of emotions, stereotyping of particular groups, or offensiveness to social values, are criticised as involving either state paternalism or censorship (or both). In addition to the general criticism that such regulation is a paternalistic interference with individual preferences, there is often the further insinuation that proponents of regulation are both elitist and anti-democratic, exhibiting contempt for popular taste and culture. Milton and Rose Friedman argue that "the real objection of most critics of advertising is not that advertising manipulates tastes but that the public at large has meretricious tastes—that is, tastes that do not agree with the critics."[10] The critic of advertising runs the danger of being characterised either as a Puritan or a socialist remnant of the "Nanny State".[11]

---

[9] *Virginia State Board of Pharmacy v. Virginia Citizens Consumer Council, Inc.* 425 U.S. 748 (1976) Blackmun J. noted a First Amendment right to receive information and ideas.

[10] M. Friedman and R. Friedman, *Free to Choose* (1980), p. 266. Perhaps they had in mind the following comment from the *Report of the Committee on The Future of Broadcasting* (1977) at para. 12.20: "Commercials which fail to sell the product are bad enough; but commercials which disfigure the screen are a disgrace. Some of us regard as odious the habit of associating aspects of life which can arouse reverence—religion, classical music and other fine arts in particular—with commercial objects of comparatively trivial benefit".

[11] In a famous article in 1948 Ralph Brown commented wryly that "anyone who questions the untrammelled use of influence by the seller and its uncoerced acceptance

This paradigm of public policy discourse reflects what might loosely be called values of liberal individualism in which the central issues are characterised as those of individual freedom versus paternalism and private markets versus public regulation.[12] This characterisation has surfaced repeatedly in constitutional discussions of the protection of advertising as commercial speech.[13] Within this approach there is room for the protection of vulnerable groups against exploitation[14] but even here the issue of paternalism is likely to be raised.[15]

There is also a preference in this approach for the use of empirical social science techniques to measure the effects of advertising. This is viewed as the most important aid to decision makers in cases where there may be difficult questions of judgment as to the impact of advertising on consumer behaviour. This preference was based on the belief that scientific analysis would provide a firm ground for policy. While there might remain ideological disagreements over the role of advertising, social science could narrow the range of disagreement and separate tractable policy issues from those which reflected individual value judgments and dogma. Empirical research could subject such "dogma and speculation" about

---

by the buyer is at best a Puritan, at worst a Fascist." R. Brown, "Advertising and the Public Interest: Legal Protection of Trade Symbols" (1948) Yale L.J. 1165 at 1181.

[12] There are differing varieties of liberalism but I believe that my description does capture that form of liberalism which has dominated legal and public policy discourse in this area. For example, Craswell in developing a normative theory of deceptive advertising argues that his theory is compatible with liberal theories of individualism and freedom. "[M]ost liberal political theories posit that individuals should be allowed to reach their own decisions, free from state intervention restricting the decision making process". R. Craswell, "Interpreting Deceptive Advertising" (1985) 65 *B.U.L. Rev.* 657 at 664.

[13] See, *e.g.* Blackmun J. in *Virginia Board of Pharmacy*, above n. 9, who characterised the justifications for restrictions on advertising of prescription drugs as "highly paternalistic" and indicated that the alternative "is to assume that this information is not in itself harmful, that people will perceive their own interests if only they are well enough informed, and that the best means to that end is to open the channels of communication rather than to close them". In his dissent in *Posadas de Puerto Rico v. Tourism Co. of Puerto Rico* 478 U.S. 328 (1986) Blackmun J. described the prohibition on advertising of gambling to residents of Puerto Rico as "a covert attempt by the State to manipulate the choices of its citizens" and an attempt "to manipulate private behaviour by depriving citizens of truthful information concerning lawful activities". See also *44 Liquor Mart v. Rhode Island Liquor Stores* 116 S. Ct. 1495 (1996) Stevens J. at 1511: "... a state legislature does not have the broad discretion to suppress truthful, nonmisleading information for paternalistic purposes...".

[14] See, *e.g.* in Europe the decision of the European Court of Justice of Case 382/87, *Buet*: [1989] E.C.R. 1235 (protection of vulnerable justifies ban on selling encyclopaedias door-to-door).

[15] Robert Pitofsky argues in an influential article that "charges that an ad, though not deceptive, tends to take advantage of a vulnerable group will usually raise controversial questions of government paternalism." R. Pitofsky, "Beyond Nader: Consumer Protection and the Regulation of Advertising" (1977) 90 *Harv. L. Rev.* 661 at 684.

advertising to the scrutiny of science.[16] This preference was most marked in relation to administrative regulation in the USA, but courts have also turned to empirical evidence on topics such as advertising to children and the regulation of tobacco advertising.[17] This preference for science also had the consequence that where the harm from advertising was not easily amenable to measurement there was a tendency to presume that, until this harm could be measured, there should be a presumption against intervention in the market. At most, the lighter touch of self-regulation, such as that of the U.K. Advertising Standards Authority was the preferred instrument in these situations.

The dominance of this common sense has eclipsed other traditions in advertising law, namely truth in advertising and advertising as manipulation. Truth in advertising envisaged an important role for law as an ethical critique of market excesses and the culture of market behaviour. Advertising as manipulation viewed advertising as a potentially wasteful form of marketing activity which undermined rational consumer decision making. Both these traditions have influenced legislation and judicial decision making. The idea of truth in advertising forms a basis for the English *Trade Descriptions Act* 1968. Some of the most celebrated U.S. consumer law and products liability cases imposed liability on manufacturers based partly on the power of advertising to manipulate consumer behaviour.[18] The economic concept of artificial product differentiation, where advertisers use brand and image advertising to create illusory differences between similar or the same products is an important

---

[16] See M. Trebilcock et al., *A Study on Consumer Misleading and Unfair Trade Practices* (1976), p. 29.

[17] See below, pp. 98–118.

[18] In his famous concurring judgment in *Escola v. Coca Cola Bottling Co.* 150 P. 2d. 436 (Cal. 1944) Traynor J., at 433, claimed that advertising had a "lulling" effect on consumers, leading them to mis-estimate product risks.

The role of advertising by mass manufacturers to stimulate consumer demand was an important underpinning for the extension of direct liability by a manufacturer to the ultimate consumer. In *Henningsen v. Bloomfield Motors* 161 A. 2d. 68 (SCNJ, 1960) Francis J. took judicial notice of the "large scale advertising by the automobile manufacturers in television, radio, newspapers and magazines to persuade the public to buy their products" and in *Randy Knitwear v. American Cyanamid* 181 N.E. 2d 399 (New York Ct. of Appeals 1962), decided in 1962, Fuld J. commented that "the world of merchandising is no longer a world of direct contract: it is rather, a world of advertising. [Today] ... the significant warranty ... which effectively induces the purchase, is frequently that given by the manufacturer through mass advertising."

A 1961 judgment described the consumer as "bewitched, bewildered and bedevilled by glittering packaging" noting that the item selected was likely to be "the one which was so glowingly described by a glamorous television artist on the housewife's favourite program, just preceding the shopping trip". *Hamon v. Digliani* Supreme Court of Connecticut 174 A. 2d. 294 (1961). See M. Shapo, *Products Liability and the search for Justice*, Chap. 5 and "Note: Harnessing Madison Avenue: Advertising and Products Liability Theory" (1993) 107 *Harv. L. R.* 895.

example of this theory of preference manipulation. In addition, theories of emotional exploitation were developed by the U.S. Federal Trade Commission in relation to advertising which exploited parental concerns for the proper upbringing of their children.[19] This narrative suggested that advertising was part of an authoritative production system where producers could manipulate consumer desire and undermine consumer rationality.[20] Consumers were constructed as credulous (often with highly gendered overtones) and consumption was often associated implicitly with supposed feminine attributes of passivity and frivolity.

There is, therefore, a tension in the law between the currently dominant vision of the consumer as a rational subject making careful informed choices and the consumer as an object of manipulation.[21] These three approaches: advertising as information, truth in advertising and advertising as manipulation, represent the three major traditions of regulation. They draw the boundaries of law's "truth" about advertising. I mean by "truth" an authoritative discourse which claims to identify the relevant issues, procedures, and approaches for understanding the power and effect of advertising.[22]

I explore the limits of these three approaches and argue for a different perspective on the power of advertising by drawing on various strands of cultural studies. The area of cultural studies has often focused on everyday cultural practices, such as watching television, shopping and taken-for-granted behaviour such as reading advertising messages, and their relationship to broader questions concerning the relations of power in society. An early text, Richard Hoggart's *The Uses of Literacy* (1958) was a study of the relationship of the new practices and institutions associated with the growth of consumer culture in England after the Second World War and their impact on working-class culture in England. The concept of cultural power operating through

---

[19] In a case brought against ITT Continental Baking for advertisements for Wonderbread, the Commission argued that the advertisements exploited "the emotional concern of ... parents for the healthy physical and mental growth and development of their children". See *Re ITT Continental Baking Co., Inc et al.* 83 F.T.C. 865 (1973) at 876. A complaint brought against advertising for a stimulant which was headed "One Day it dawned on me that I was boring my husband to death", argued that the advertisers had represented that use of the stimulant would make one more attractive, improve one's personality, marriage and sex-life and that this was false. See *J. B. Williams Co. Inc. et al.* 81 F.T.C. 238 (1972) at 241–242.

[20] See, *e.g.* Dickson C. J. in *Irwin Toy v. Quebec (A.-G.)* [1989] 1 S.C.R. 927 at 990 where he refers to children as "particularly vulnerable to the techniques of seduction and manipulation abundant in advertising" and refers to "media manipulation".

[21] For further analysis of images of the consumer in consumer policy see, T. Wilhelmsson, "Consumer Images in East and West" in H. W. Micklitz (Hrsg.) *Rechtseinheit oder Rechtsvielfalt in Europa?* (1996), pp. 53–65.

[22] M. Foucault, *Power/Knowledge: Selected Interviews and Other Writings 1972–77* (trans. C. Gordon, 1980), p. 132.

everyday discourses and representations, such as advertising, has been greatly enriched during the past few decades by the analyses of Foucault, feminist theory and writers such as Edward Said who have demonstrated the power of cultural discourse and representations in sustaining domination and oppressive social relations. This conception of power does not operate from above, as suggested by manipulation theory which assumes the consumer to be a puppet of commercial power. It is rather a power which circulates throughout society and which shapes individuals' sense of themselves and their relations to others. Discourses which continually invite us to view social relations from the viewpoint of a consumer, rather than a producer or citizen, shape individual and social life. Feminist theory has examined the role of powerful normalising discourses, such as those reflected in advertising, in continually inviting women to "buy in" to oppressive images of femininity and beauty practices.

This shaping of consciousness through everyday practices cannot be equated with simple ideas of manipulation but it also denies the idea that individuals are autonomous individuals with pre-existing identities who make free choices. Cultural studies draws attention to a crucial fact that in the consumer markets of consumer capitalism there is an inextricable linking of culture and economy, and advertising provides the link between culture and economy. Markets cannot be adequately understood as merely economic phenomena. If consumer culture may be a site for the reproduction of relations of inequality and subordination in society, then a further question has been to understand when and why individuals challenge rather than reproduce these social relations. The culture of media consumerism is viewed as a site not merely for shaping identities but also for contesting and challenging dominant social ideologies. This politicised conception of the supposedly private world of consumer market relations under-lines the important mediating role of culture between economic power and social action and suggests a modification of theories which assumed that the central location of conflict in society was around work and production relations.

Law is, like advertising, a significant narrative which represents and con-stitutes the social world through its conception of the legal subject. The reasonable person of the law is one of the best known examples of this process. Consumer law constructs the subject of consumer law through such discourses as the distinction between the reasonable and credulous consumer in the field of misleading advertising law. These representations may be a significant aspect of culture and the narratives of the law are important sources of official values, that in turn influence conceptions of how individuals see themselves and relationships in society.[23] Law provides also a potential source of critique of these relations and this symbolic role of state law may be of as great significance

---

[23] See discussion of this topic in relation to contract law in R. Gordon, "Macaulay Macneil and the discovery of solidarity and power in contract law" (1985) *Wisconsin L. Rev.* 565.

Chapter 2

Law's Truth and Advertising: Three Narratives

This chapter explores three narratives in advertising law: truth in advertising, advertising as information and advertising as preference manipulation. The currently dominant approach, particularly in North America,[1] conceptualises advertising as information, but there is a continuing tension between these narratives, and each is best understood in terms of its relationship to the other. The strands of these narratives may be found, not only in consumer law, but also in competition law, trademark law and constitutional adjudication on freedom of speech. An exploration of these narratives reveals differing visions of consumer markets, consumers and the role of law as a critique of market behaviour. They illustrate how law has constituted the subject of consumer law and the relation of this construction to ideologies of consumer protection and to social divisions of class, gender and race. As we shall see the subject of consumer law retains many of the characteristics of the liberal legal subject.[2] Although consumer law grew as a critique of classical contract law with its liberal assumptions of rational and formally equal subjects, it has not, in the area of advertising law, shaken loose from its origins as merely an exception to these assumptions. By retaining many of the dualisms of liberal legal thought consumer law has been blunted as a critique of consumer capitalism.[3]

---

[1] Thomas Wilhelmsson has drawn my attention to the fact that this approach may be less dominant in Germany and Scandinavia.

[2] See below, pp. 70–86.

[3] For a discussion of these dualisms as hierarchically ordered dualisms which reflect gendered distinctions such as rational/male: irrational/female see F. Olsen, "The Sex of Law" in *The Politics of Law* (D. Kairys ed., 2nd ed., 1990), p. 453.

For these reasons, these narratives are limited in their conceptualisation of the power of advertising and in furthering dialogue on the nature of advertising in society. This chapter provides a prologue to subsequent chapters which examine advertising as an aspect of cultural domination, and reassess legal doctrines in the light of cultural studies.

1 Truth in Advertising

The idea of truth in advertising is based on an ethical critique of lying in the marketplace and the potentially corrosive impact of such behaviour on social values. It is not concerned solely with assessing the consequential costs of inaccurate information on consumer choice. As the *Review of Legislation on False and Misleading Price Information* noted, the central reason for regulation of such claims does "not depend upon the harm which such information may cause him [the consumer] but on the moral argument that the provision of false and misleading information is in itself wrong".[4] Movements for truth in advertising, such as that associated with the U.S. progressive period of the early twentieth century, have often been critiques of the moral order of the existing ground rules of consumer markets and, when expressed through the law, they are attempts to influence cultural values. When a Canadian judge stated in 1970 that "to allow a producer to evade the fair implications of his advertising is to permit him to reap a rich harvest of profit without obligation to the purchaser. ... Honesty in advertising is a concept worthy of re-examination," he was not merely speaking to other judges.[5] As we shall see below, truth in advertising is currently criticised as (1) a meaningless concept in a world of polysemic advertising texts where consumers purchase images and signs rather than objective products, (2) a hopelessly vague guide for public policy and (3) a reflection of a literal-minded puritanism. Yet there remains a remarkable level of lies in the consumer marketplace and I shall argue that truth may still be an important cultural value in the constitution of consumer markets.

---

[4] *Review of Legislation on False and Misleading Price Information: Report on the Interdepartmental Working Party* (1984), p. 20.
[5] *Ranger v. Herbert A. Watts (Quebec) Ltd. et al.* (1970) 10 D.L.R. (3d) 395, Haines J. at 405.

Truth in advertising seems a relatively modest objective for a consumer market, but it is an objective which has been criticised by many as an ineffective method of addressing the power of advertising in consumer capitalism. An initial critique points to the difficulties of separating truth and falsity in much modern advertising. One does not need to subscribe to post-modern epistemological scepticism to realise that the texts and images of advertising copy may be interpreted in several differing ways. Innuendo, exaggeration and ambiguity are its stock-in-trade. In addition, an unremitting quest for truth, such as a requirement that "Vienna Rolls" should come from Vienna, can also be portrayed as literal-minded legalism which is only likely to protect a few "misguided souls"[6] from deception. Much advertising invites us to buy images. If consumers purchase signs and images and construct lifestyles from signs associated with products, it becomes difficult to state that images are false since reality is constructed through the images and their interpretation by consumers.

Certain law and economics scholars, as we discuss in the next section, have exploited these difficulties to argue that the objective in regulating deceptive advertising should not be truth but rather that of assuring a reliable market for information, taking into account the costs and benefits of regulation. If the costs of reducing deception outweigh the benefits (for example because they result in less information being conveyed to a majority of consumers) then the advertisements should not be proscribed.

A second criticism is that the focus on truth and falsity in modern advertising is attacking the periphery not the core. Most of modern advertising invites consumers to purchase images and fantasies associated with the product, rather than merely the product itself, but the law still focuses on the use value of the product. On this view, the law

---

[6] See *Heinz W. Kirchner Re*, 63 F.T.C. 1282 (1963) at 1290 where the Federal Trade Commission addressed a claim that a swimming aid to be worn under a swimming suit was "thin and invisible". In fact it was not invisible and so was a false statement. Commissioner Elman noted that it was unlikely that many prospective purchasers would take the representation in its literal sense and commented that although the Commission's responsibility was to protect deception of the gullible

"[t]his principle loses its validity, however, if it is applied uncritically or pushed to an absurd extreme. An advertiser cannot be charged with liability with respect of every conceivable misconception, however outlandish, to which his representations might be subject among the foolish or feeble-minded ... Perhaps a few misguided souls would believe, for example, that all 'Danish pastry' is made in Denmark. Is it therefore an actual deception to advertise 'Danish pastry' when it is made in this country? Of course not."

is out of touch with the realities of modern advertising, "an archaic reminder of an earlier historical epoch when commodities were presented as possessing straightforward use values and exchange values".[7] This criticism is not new. Aldous Huxley argued that there existed "the development of a vast mass communications industry, concerned in the main with neither the true nor the false, but with the unreal".[8] In 1970 Trebilcock argued that "[t]he law has been slow to catch up with the realities of modern advertising. Even today the burning question in law reform circles still seems to be, what is to be done about false and deceptive advertising in the traditional sense of those terms".[9] Patricia Williams echoes these sentiments 20 years later stating that at one time:

> "the mathematics of false advertising was simple. If the box or brochure said '100% Cotton' you merely took the item in question and subtracted it from the words: any difference was the measure of your legal remedy ... Today, however, advertisers almost never represent anything remotely related to the reality of the product ... they are trying to sell ... What fills the sixty seconds are 'concepts' and diffuse images".[10]

She also argues that private law may be out of touch with modern image marketing. The concept of "reasonable fitness for purpose" evokes concepts of utility but how would it apply to a T-shirt which had inadvertently omitted the manufacturer's logo (such as Benetton, or Gap)?

It is undoubtedly the case that much of modern advertising invites the consumer to enjoy a lifestyle or identify with a group through the purchase of a product. The image and lifestyle advertisements are the modern versions of the advertising "puff" which traditionally gave rise to no liability. The law's common sense has drawn a distinction between the "mere puff" for which there is no liability and statements making factual claims which might give rise to liability if they are false and misleading. The modern rationale for this puffing immunity is that no person would take puffs seriously and they are too vague and subjective

---

[7] R. Goldman, *Reading Ads Socially* (1992), p. 83.

[8] A. Huxley, *Brave New World Revisited* quoted in R. Collins and D. Skover, "The Death of Discourse" in Winter (1996) *Adbusters* 11.

[9] M. Trebilcock, "Consumer Protection in the Affluent Society" (1970) 16 *McGill L.J.* 263 at 282.

[10] Patricia Williams, *The Alchemy of Race and Rights* (1991), at 36–37.

to represent any factual product claim.[11] The law assumes that the
rational consumer will discount the image that "Coke adds life" and
make a rational choice based on the factual attributes of the product.
The historical roots of the puffing doctrine are in the nineteenth
century. With characteristic confidence Mr Justice Holmes stated in
1889 that:

> "It is settled that the law does not exact good faith from a seller in those
> vague commendations of his wares which manifestly are open to difference
> of opinion, — which do not imply untrue assertions concerning matters of
> direct observation, ... and as to which it always has been understood, the
> world over, that such statements are to be distrusted".[12]

For Holmes the puff seemed to represent a culturally accepted ritual
of negotiation where all market transactions begin based on distrust
and a social ritual of exaggeration. Perhaps the assumption was of the
puff as the beginning of negotiations, the opening gambit to be followed
by more serious negotiations.

Another famous U.S. judge, Learned Hand commented that:

> "There are some kinds of talk which no sensible man takes seriously, and if
> he does he suffers from his own credulity. If we were all scrupulously honest
> it would not be so; but, as it is, neither party usually believes what the seller
> says about his own opinions, and each knows it. Such statements, like the
> statements of campaign managers before elections, are rather designed to
> allay the suspicion which would attend their absence than to be understood
> as having any relation to objective truth".[13]

The cultural vision of market behaviour in Holmes' and Hand's

---

[11] See R. Pitofsky, "Beyond Nader: Consumer Protection and The Regulation of
Advertising" (1977) 90 *Harv. L. Rev.* 661.

[12] *Deming v. Darling* 20 N.E. 107 (1889) at 108. See Walton J. in *De Beers Abrasive Products
Ltd v. International General Electric Co. of N.Y. Ltd* [1975] 1 W.L.R. 972. "In other words
in the kind of situation where one expects, as a matter of ordinary common experience,
a person to use a certain amount of hyperbole in the description of goods, property
or services, the courts will do what any ordinary reasonable man would do, namely,
take it with a large pinch of salt".

[13] *Vulcan Metals Co. v. Simmons Mfg. Co.* 248 F. 853 (2d. Cir. 1918) at 856. Note that the
context of this case may have been significant. It concerned the sale of a business
between two knowledgeable parties and Hand commented that the issue might have
been different between a manufacturer and a consumer where the parties are not
meeting on equal terms.

rhetoric seems far removed from the sophisticated image marketing of contemporary marketing. Many advertisements present images of the relationship which one may expect with the advertiser. One does not buy a discrete product but the relationship. Insurance companies and financial institutions stress the image of trust, and credit card companies underline the social distinction attached to their cards. Other images in the advertisement will represent particular interpretations of social life and relationships which the consumer is invited to identify with the product. The images are often offering commodified solutions to individual problems, suggesting appropriate ways of living, and ways of looking at ourselves and others. In these cases there is no clear separation between the object of the sale and the image.

Consider in this context the following story:

> "In May, Michigan Court of Appeals affirmed a lower court decision dismissing Richard Overton's $10,000 lawsuit against Anheuser Busch for false advertising. Overton said he suffered physical and mental injury and emotional distress because the implicit promises in the company's advertisements, especially of success with women, did not come true for him when he drank their product, and that besides that he sometimes got sick when he drank". *Toronto Star* July 23, 1994.

Mr Overton's suit is not another apocryphal example of the supposed U.S. litigation explosion.[14] He had claimed that television advertisements for Bud Light misled the public because they were the source of fantasies coming to life, "fantasies involving tropical settings, and beautiful women and men engaged in unrestricted merriment".[15] The Michigan Court of Appeals concluded that the idea of fantasies coming to life was a grandiose suggestion and constituted puffing. One might speculate on the reaction of commentators to a successful suit against Anheuser Busch on the basis that the advertisements were misleading because he did not in fact achieve "success with women" after drinking the beer. I suspect that a common sense reaction might be that no fool would believe the literal truth of the advertisement. Indeed the fact that this case is in the newspaper is simply a further example of the bizarre types of litigation indulged in by certain parts of the U.S. population. Everyone knows that these are "just images" used to sell

---

[14] See *Overton v. Anheuser Busch* 517 N.W. 2d. 308 (1994).
[15] *ibid.*, at 309.

products. Although the Advertising Standards Authority in the United Kingdom states that "[a]dvertisements should not suggest that any alcoholic drink can enhance mental, physical or sexual capabilities, popularity, attractiveness, masculinity . . ." this has done little to prevent subtle lifestyle advertising of alcoholic products.

Susan Bordo makes the following comments about the reactions of some of her students when she interprets the meaning of the images of ads as carrying deeply sedimented and damaging cultural images of women:

> "Students accuse me of a kind of paranoia about the significance of these representations as carriers and reproducers of culture. After all, they insist, these are just images, not 'real life'; any fool knows that advertisers manipulate reality in the service of selling their products".[16]

But if consumption is as much an idealist as a material practice, and if "reality" is a cultural construct where individuals shape their shifting identities in the field of consumption, should we dismiss so swiftly the significance of these claims as "mere" puffs?

Bordo puts the issue more bluntly in the sentence following the above:

> "I agree that on some level we 'know' this [that the advertisements are just images]. However, were it a meaningful or usable knowledge, it is unlikely that we would be witnessing the current spread of diet and exercise mania across racial and ethnic groups."

The phrase: "Were it a meaningful or usable knowledge" seems to tap into the power and authority of advertising. The idea that consumption is a rational process where individuals separate the symbolic fantasies from the rational use value of the product, discounting the former before making a rational choice, does not seem to describe accurately much of modern consumption behaviour. Individuals may "buy in" to images even though they are aware that they are just images. Individuals may not necessarily buy the product but the saturation of the secondary messages of advertising—which portray particular social relations, measures of success and the continuing importance of commodity pur-

---

[16] S. Bordo, *Unbearable Weight: Feminism, Western Culture and the Body* (1993), p. 104.

chasing—are likely to shape consciousness and behaviour. The recognition that consumption is an idealist as well as a material practice is not novel. Bordo's argument is that this "buying in" to images of personal and social relations is not necessarily an innocent affair in a society with a long cultural history of the subordination and oppression of women. Returning to Mr Overton's case, the portrayal in much beer advertising of images of women as young, white, and stereotypically attractive may be merely "fantasy" but it is argued that such images have significant harmful effects (see below, Chapter 3) on women. Advertisements for beer are not just selling beer, but images of men, women and social relationships. The product is an appendage to these images, suggesting that it is in fact the puff/image which is the core of the advertisement.

Images in advertising may be taken very seriously by consumers. Consider the case of GAP, the international clothes retailer. It had carefully cultivated a "cool" image among young consumers. In 1995 it was revealed that GAP used sweated labour, working under appalling conditions in El Salvador. This resulted in significant pressures from both labour, consumer and student groups on GAP who agreed to provide for better conditions and monitoring of those conditions by a third party. Part of the outrage experienced by young consumers was their realisation of the contrast between the image and the reality of the company. This example also suggests that the contrast between image and reality may have a more material basis than suggested by more extreme writers on the consumer society who appear to argue that reality is merely a socially constructed series of discourses.

Images may be open to different interpretations, but there seems no reason in principle why the law could not scrutinise them more closely. I indicated that many financial institutions stress the importance of the relationship of trust and confidence which they wish to develop with consumers and this is part of their advertising image. Buying "a piece of the Rock" is merely one example of the genre. It is often a carefully constructed part of the culture of financial markets. It does not seem far-fetched to argue that these images and stories may raise consumer expectations that they will be treated fairly. Traditional contract law however sent a differing cultural message to consumers: don't trust anyone; read the small print; get advice and don't believe the puff. But consumers who do behave as this model suggests would probably be regarded as exceptional, if not somewhat odd,consumers.

Modern writers on contract have developed a relational theory of contracting which emphasises the importance of "relational norms" such as trust and co-operation which arise in many forms of modern contracting.[17] English law has been slow to recognise these norms in a consumer setting or to acknowledge the relational role of company images in advertising. U.S. courts have shown greater willingness to cite consumer trust encouraged by advertising images as one reason for holding a manufacturer directly liable to a consumer for unsafe products and insurance companies liable in punitive damages for bad faith behaviour. As one judge stated: "This case can be summed up as follows: Plaintiff at the inducement of the Prudential, got herself 'a piece of the rock', and now that it's time for the insurance company to pay, Prudential wants to take its rocks and go home".[18] The concept of damages for emotional distress could also be based on these breaches of consumer trust.

A second issue raised by the puffing image is whether analysis of these images should always be viewed through the lens of truth and falsity. A different approach might be to argue that they may raise questions of exploitation and unfairness, which traditionally the law has been slow to recognise. This approach would require attention to the social and cultural context of the transmission and receipt of particular advertising images, and possibly the development of a differ- ent vision of the consumer than the rational choice model implicit in the law. It would also require the development of a critique of routine practices of advertising and common sense assumptions that "no one takes seriously puffing images". The legal model of rational-choice assumes that consumers buy products based on an assessment of their factual or objective attributes and that consumers who do not follow this model may be characterised as irrational shoppers. Buying images is irrational behaviour. This approach by the law courts the danger of not taking seriously the role of consumption as an idealist practice. The contrast of reason/emotion in the rational/irrational distinction, with its gendered overtones, raises questions about masculinist bias in the law. Law constructs the shopper who "buys into" fantasies as representing

---

[17] A useful summary of the relational traditions may be found in R. Gordon, "Macaulay, Macneil, and the Discovery of Solidarity and Power in Contract Law" (1985) *Wisconsin L. Rev.* 565.

[18] *Irion v. Prudential Ins. Co.* 765 F. Supp. 337, 388n.2 (N.D. Texas 1991) cited in T. Baker, "Constructing the Insurance Relationship: Sales Stories, Claims Stories, and Insurance Contract Damages" (1994) 72 *Texas L. R.* 1395 at n. 7 and see also M. Shapo, *op. cit.*, Chap. 1, n. 18.

supposed feminine impulsiveness and gullibility, historically associated
with consumption markets.[19]

Notwithstanding the comments of critics such as Trebilcock and
Williams, I believe that the discourse of truth remains important as a
cultural critique of advertising practices. There remains a remarkable
amount of straightforward fraud and lying in the consumer marketplace.
In Canada there are 14,000 complaints annually to the Federal auth-
orities concerning misleading advertising. In addition, it is a useful
exercise to draw attention to such truths as the fact that while most
advertising to children in North America addresses a viewer who is
implicitly WASP, male and middle class, "most children in the United
States are poor, ethnic, and female".[20] This is a material fact and an
important form of criticism remains that of drawing attention to
distinctions between ideology and reality. There remains also an important material aspect to consumption. There are real distinctions between
products which are not merely social constructions or images. It might
be a novel marketing image to market a new mineral water as eau
sulphurique but if the bottles contained sulphuric acid the images would
not save the consumers from the grave.

The concept of truth also recognises the value in holding consumer
markets to relatively high ethical standards and attempting to maintain
a moral order in the market.[21] This may affect the culture of the
market, something which consumers may be unable to do individually.
This is regarded as a crucial objective in other markets, such as
securities markets, which are still populated primarily by affluent
consumers. In discussing rules for derivatives trading, a Bank of America
official stated that "[a]rms length does not mean laissez-faire ... it is
not buyer beware. The wholesale financial markets are not used car
markets."[22] There is encapsulated here a cultural vision of the moralities
of different markets. It is assumed that the culture of the used car

---

[19] See generally J. Lears, *Fables of Abundance: A Cultural History of Advertising in America*
(1995).

[20] E. Seiter, *Sold Separately: Children and Parents in Consumer Culture* (1995), p. 230.

[21] For the concept of regulation as a method of maintaining moral order in markets see
J. Burk, *Values in the Marketplace: The American Stock Market under Federal Securities Law*
(1988), pp. 7–17. See also, M. Granovetter, "Economic Action and Social Structure:
The Problem of Embeddedness" (1985) 91 *American Journal of Sociology* 482.

[22] Lewis Teel, Bank of America Vice-President and Chair, New York Federal Reserve
Board foreign exchange committee, which helped to draft industry rules on derivative
products, quoted in Toronto *Globe and Mail*, August 19, 1995.

market is something which consumers take for granted and presumably enjoy. But there is nothing natural about the cultural rituals of buying and selling cars and there is evidence that consumers do not enjoy the culture of this market.[23] The discourse of truth remains, therefore, as a valuable critique of the culture of markets. The economic objection to this approach is that the pursuit of truth may result in less information being provided to consumers. Whether this is a significant issue is discussed in the following section.

2 Advertising as Information[24]

This approach rejects the ethical norm of truth as an objective for regulation. In the words of Pitofsky's influential article, "[p]rotection of consumers against advertising fraud should not be a broad, theoretical effort to achieve Truth, but rather a practical enterprise to ensure the existence of reliable data which in turn will facilitate an efficient and reliable competitive market process."[25] Regulation is a response to failures in markets for information. This approach drew on the neo-classical economic analysis of the role of information in markets which had begun with Stigler's article in 1961.[26] This approach assumes that information is a cost of transacting and that consumers may face differing search costs for information. A rational consumer will search until the marginal costs of further search exceed the marginal costs. Consumers may also obtain information through experience and some low cost products such as chocolate bars may only be tested through experience. However, some infrequently purchased products may have experience qualities (the comfort of an automobile) and consumers may turn to third parties for information on these characteristics. Sellers will also have incentives to provide consumers with information and may

---

[23] For evidence of sexual and racial discrimination in this market see I. Ayres, "Fair Driving: Gender and Race Discrimination in Retail Car Negotiations" (1991) 104 *Harv. L. R.* 817.

[24] The next two sections draw on my article "Advertising, Taste Construction and the Search for Enlightened Policy: A Critique" (1991) 29 *Osgoode Hall L. J.* 573.

[25] R. Pitofsky, "Beyond Nader: Consumer Protection and the Regulation of Advertising" (1977) 90 Harv. L. R. 661 at 671.

[26] G. Stigler, "The Economics of Information" (1961) 69 *Journal of Political Economy* 213.

do so through information signals such as warranties or reputation. Much of the law and economics of information is directed towards identifying those situations where this market information process breaks down. Since no market is likely to have perfect information, the task for the policymaker is to identify those market situations which are likely to produce information failures and where consumers may have difficulties in protecting themselves. For example, door-to-door sales or telemarketing often involve selling where the seller is not interested in the consumer as a repeat-player and will invest resources in overcoming a consumer's resistance through high pressure selling. It may be more difficult for consumers to assess experience qualities such as the precise impact of a water softener on the water quality and so there may be here a rationale for regulation.

One consequence of this form of analysis was a rejection of the idea that deceptive advertising was bad *per se*. This conclusion was based on several grounds. First, consumers might well be able to protect themselves against deceptive claims in many product markets. This might include deceptive pricing of low cost, frequently purchased, products where consumers faced low costs in comparing prices. Secondly, the concept of deception was not straightforward. Almost any advertisement might deceive some consumers. The issue of deception could not be separated from the larger question of the whole information environment of a market and the costs and benefits of targeting different types of claims. Prohibition of deceptive claims might actually be counterproductive since it could reduce levels of market information which might be useful to those consumers who were not deceived. The assumption was that protection of credulous consumers, as in the earlier "Vienna rolls" example, might restrict information to reasonable consumers. While there might be equitable grounds for protecting this group, it was important to indicate the economic costs to those deprived of information. In short, the analysis accepted a normative cost-benefit approach to deceptive advertising.

The conception of advertising as information also challenged the distinction between informative (good) and persuasive (bad) advertising by pointing out that all advertising provided some information, *e.g.* that a product exists and that much advertising of low-priced products was of the "try me" category.[27] Images and puffs were simply attention

---

grabbing messages. This approach challenged earlier economic conceptions of advertising which had often viewed advertising as a wasteful contribution to market segmentation and associated with unnecessary proliferation and differentiation of products. Writing in 1977 Ronald Coase argued that economists had until "comparatively recently ... tended to deplore rather than analyse the effects of advertising. In recent years, advertising has been studied more rigorously and this has been accompanied by, or perhaps we should say has resulted in, a more sympathetic attitude to advertising".[28]

This approach rejected, therefore, the idea of law as a critique of market behaviour. Law merely addressed information failures. It substituted the supposedly weak value judgments embedded in the norm of consumer sovereignty in welfare economics and transformed a moral and political issue into the more manageable policy question of technical and empirical analysis. "Intervention" in the economy was necessary to merely make a central social institution work more effectively. It did not seem to involve the overruling of consumer preferences or government paternalism. The normative basis of regulation was to aid free decision-making and information remedies are the primary remedy for market problems with information. Beales, Craswell and Salop state explicitly the values underlying this approach:

"Remedies which simply adjust the information available to consumers still leave consumers free to make their own choices ... in short, information remedies allow consumers to protect themselves according to personal preferences rather than place on regulators the difficult task of compromising diverse preferences with a common standard".[29]

The economic approach to advertising as information has become influential in policy-making, most notably at the U.S. Federal Trade Commission, and has seeped into constitutional discourse through the commercial speech doctrine. It would be churlish to deny its value in consumer protection. It formed the basis for the development of legal doctrines of advertising substantiation, corrective advertising, required disclosures and other information remedies. There are, however, limitations in this approach. First, it has not proved a simple task to identify

---

[28] See R. Coase, "Advertising and Free Speech" (1977) 6 *Journal of Leg. Studies* 1 at 8–9.
[29] H. Beales, R. Craswell and S. Salop, "The Efficient Regulation of Consumer Information" (1981) 24 *Journal of Law and Economics* 491 at 514.

with empirical precision those market situations where intervention is justified. A leading article on the economics of information concludes that "it is extremely difficult to develop many hard-and-fast rules and the proper policy to be followed will depend heavily on the facts of each case.[30] Posner and Pitofsky diverge significantly in their assessment of the need for government regulation of misleading advertising, notwithstanding that both authors adopt a market failure approach to regulation.

Secondly, the normative basis of this approach remains to correct preferences in order to achieve more rational consumer decision-making. It is assumed that, but for the misleading information, consumers would have revealed differing preferences which they would have preferred to those based on misleading information. Such a counterfactual argument might, however, be extended to a wide variety of potential beliefs induced by advertising which leads to irrational behaviour. Resistance to this potential slippery slope is based on the arguments that false factual beliefs are more easily established and do not require controversial value judgments about the worth of preferences. *De Gustibus non est disputandum.* Craswell argues that "there is no widely shared definition of a rational decision making process. The distinction between rational and irrational is much harder to define than the distinction between true or false".[31] The fact remains, however, that this approach avoids the question of the extent to which market behaviour is shaped by particular economic and cultural structures and fails to acknowledge that the law itself may play a role in this shaping process. The role of regulation in the information approach is not to transform preferences, merely to follow.

Thirdly, generalisations about the importance of advertising as information to market efficiency tend to be based on empirical studies of a limited number of markets, such as those for the sale of eyeglasses and professional services, where advertising had been prohibited.[32] These markets may not resemble many other standard consumer product markets, such as breakfast cereals, cosmetics, clothing, and pharmaceuticals, which are dominated by multinational firms which gather vast volumes of data on consumer preferences and tastes. The limited

---

[30] *ibid.*, at 532.
[31] R. Craswell, "Interpreting Deceptive Advertising" (1985) 65 B.U.L. Rev. 657.
[32] See, *e.g.* L. Benham, "The Effect of Advertising on the Prices of Eyeglasses" (1972) 15 *Journal of Law and Economics* 337.

studies of these markets are more equivocal about the role of advertising.[33] In addition, studies have often focused on the short term impact
of the introduction of advertising to a market and these may be of
limited value in providing information on the long term impact of
advertising on prices and quality, in shaping preferences and in reproducing and reinforcing social stereotypes.

One area where the economics of information has been influential
is that of the regulation of misleading price advertising. This issue has
generated a significant amount of interest by policymakers in North
America and Europe with contrasting policy responses. Since the mid
1960s in the USA, the Federal Trade Commission has brought almost
no actions against misleading price claims which compare the sale price
with the sellers' former regular selling price. This contrasts with Canada,
and many European countries where price advertising prosecutions
constitute a significant percentage of misleading advertising prosecutions.[34] The introduction of the moratorium at the Federal Trade
Commission was also in direct contrast to an earlier period where a
significant amount of effort was directed towards "30% off Claims" or
"lowest price in town".

The change in priorities was made under the direction of Robert
Pitofsky, head of the consumer protection branch of the agency in the
early 1970s. Pitofsky justified this approach in his subsequent article in
the *Harvard Law Review* in terms of economic analysis. He argued for
the central importance of price advertising to market competition
and the comparative advantage of consumers in assessing potentially
misleading claims. He argued that consumers were often in a good
position to check the validity of claims, were likely to ignore ambiguous
claims and would in any event often receive a bargain. There was also
a suspicion that enforcement of price advertising claims had often
responded to competitors complaints about new market entrants. Price
advertising was an important method of new firms breaking into

---

[33] See, *e.g.* M. Hurwitz and R. Caves, "Persuasion or Information? Promotion and the
Shares of Brand Names and Generic Pharmaceuticals (1988) 31 *Journal of Law and
Economics* 299.

[34] In Canada price claim prosecutions comprise over 50 per cent of the prosecutions for
misleading advertising brought by the Federal Marketing Practices Branch under s.52
of the *Federal Competition Act.* In the U.K. prosecution of misleading pricing remains a
large category of prosecutions under Pt. III of the *Consumer Protection Act* 1987. See R.
Bragg, *Trade Descriptions* (1991) Chap. 5 and I. Ramsay, *Consumer Protection* (1989) pp.
251–257.

an entrenched market. As a consequence, aggressive enforcement of ambiguous or potentially deceptive claims might dampen market competition, bar new entrants, and reduce consumer welfare. The reduction in attention to price claims would free enforcement resources to attack performance claims, such as claims relating to the stopping performance of tyres, where consumers would have difficulties in assessing performance in advance. Pitofsky provided surprisingly little data to support his arguments on price advertising, notwithstanding the fact that the article was published in the footnote-conscious *Harvard Law Review.*

There was, therefore, a moratorium on the enforcement of misleading price claims. By the late 1980s there was significant concern in relation to widespread practices of "high/low" selling, where prices were set at an artificially high price for a short period and then discounted. In addition, sales appeared to have become weekly events with over 60 per cent of department store sales volume being sold at sale prices. Lawyer/economists continued to advocate a hands-off approach to regulation, citing evidence that bans on price advertising in legal services and elsewhere had increased prices and that, echoing Pitofsky, consumers were well aware of high/low selling practices and adapted their behaviour accordingly. It was in fact suggested that consumers might stockpile sale items and defer purchases, knowing that a sale would occur.[35]

A closer examination of the price claims issue suggests that the question of regulation is complex. There is little direct empirical evidence of the effects of aggressive price regulation across a wide variety of consumer markets over the short and long term. For example, at what point does price advertising become so anarchic that the costs of comparative search become confusingly high? Does unregulated price advertising lead to new entrants or to increasing concentration in retail capital?[36] What are the distributional effects of unregulated pricing claims? Does it benefit those who have ease of access (*e.g.* through more leisure time, ownership of automobile) to increased search time? What are the implications for product quality, availability? Does it result in

---

[35] T. Muris, "Economics and Consumer Protection" (1991) 60 *Antitrust Law Journal* 115.
[36] See, *e.g.* Ducatel and Blomley, "Rethinking Retail Capital" 14 *International Journal of Urban Relations* 219. R. Bragg raises the possibility that price advertising may be used to squeeze out competitors although he indicates that "[i]n most goods categories there is little evidence that this has happened so far". R. Bragg, *Trade Descriptions* (1991) p. 85.

lower cash prices being advertised but retailers recouping margins on expensive products through credit charges (which is a common form of selling many consumer goods)?

In a study of the "high/low" pricing question Kaufman found that surveys of consumers indicated that the practices created confusion among consumers and it was difficult to determine whether these practices increased social welfare.[37] He argues that the issue of high/low pricing raises questions about differing visions of market ground rules, the role of consumers and business in gathering information, and ideas of fairness and trust in the marketplace. The practices may be contributing to the belief that the normal prices in the market are a bargain, essentially an ideological rather than realistic vision of the consumer market. The fact that consumers adapt to these practices does not indicate unambiguously that these "adaptive preferences" are really what consumers prefer.

At this point it might be useful to return to Pitofsky and the lawyer-economists. If there is not strong empirical support for Pitofsky's argument it may be that we could read his argument at another level. The image of price advertising where "the little guy" breaks into a market of entrenched sellers forcing change and innovation carries perhaps populist U.S. cultural visions of the market. Similarly, the image of the astute consumer searching out sales seems ideological rather than scientific. In this vision shopping is a game where the subversive consumer enjoys the opportunity "to outwit the economic system by spying a 'bargain' ".[38]

A different approach to the issue of regulation might be to pose the question whether it is socially desirable to structure the ground rules of a market in such a way that they require consumers to engage in potentially paranoiac searching for price bargains. The issue cannot be answered in terms of efficiency since efficiency is a relative concept. Both the Canadian and German consumer markets are efficient, in the sense of reaching a partial equilibrium, although they have greater policing of price claims than the United States. The really interesting question is what type of market will be encouraged and that seems as much a cultural or ideological question as one involving scientific

---

[37] See P. Kaufman et al., "Fairness in Consumer Pricing" (1991) 14 *Journal of Consumer Policy* 117.
[38] R. Lynd, "Democracy's Third Estate: The Consumer" (1936) *Political Science Quarterly* 481 at 492.

expertise. Perhaps it is a source of pleasure to seek out bargains, perhaps there are potential pathologies of shopping.[39] Shopping remains women's work in many countries. Most of the law and economics literature, with its assumptions about consumer stockpiles are written by men making armchair speculations about rational behaviour. Until recently, there has been no rich ethnography on this women's work in relation to consumption management.[40] In a society which wishes to transform commodity consumerism into a major part of social life, so that shopping becomes a vocation, the U.S. vision might be appropriate. Andy Warhol said that "shopping is more American than thinking". But it is hardly a non-controversial vision of social life.

The focus on advertising as information suggested that much apparently persuasive advertising, such as the attention grabbing advertisement, is really providing a consumer with information. But advertising which appears to be providing information may also be seen as persuasive and cultivating taste changes. This is illustrated by a study conducted by economists at the Federal Trade Commission. They studied the impact of lifting a regulatory ban on cereal producers highlighting the health benefits of their products and, in particular, the campaign by Kelloggs in association with The National Cancer Institute which cited links between fibre consumption and reductions in the incidence of certain cancers. The economic study showed that after the introduction of this advertising by the cereal companies there was a large increase in knowledge of the link between fibre and cancer and in fibre cereal consumption, with the largest increases among lower income populations. The authors of the study concluded that this showed the importance of advertising as a source of information and that good consumer policy "requires that we focus as much on increasing the flow of truthful information as we do on stopping deceptive or misleading claims."[41]

It is difficult to disagree with such a conclusion. But the study could also be interpreted as showing the power of advertising by companies such as Kelloggs to shape consumer preferences by playing on anxieties

---

[39] See R. Elliott, "Addictive Consumption: Function and Fragmentation in Post Modernity" (1994) 17 *Journal of Consumer Policy* 159.

[40] See now, *e.g.* M. Luxton and H. Rosenberg, *Through the Kitchen Window: The Politics of Home and Family* (1986).

[41] P. M. Ippolito and A. D. Mathios, "The Regulation of Science Based Claims in Advertising" (1990) 13 *Journal of Consumer Policy* 413 at 441.

about health, particularly among lower income populations, and suggesting that the solution is in eating breakfast cereal. Whether this is likely to be a significant long-term contribution to the public health is more debatable, given the continuing high rate of obesity among the U.S. population. Policy makers assumed that the move to consume high-fibre cereals was a *good* change. But given the effectiveness of advertising in this context one could read the study as suggesting the power of advertising to shape taste. It was not the only factor in shaping taste, but it did shape it in a particular direction, namely the consumption of breakfast cereals as the solution to concerns about cancer. The study might also be read as support for the argument that, contrary to industry protestations, the breakfast cereal industry was very effective during the post-war period at persuading children and adults to eat highly sugared cereals for breakfast for many years. But this was always rejected by the corporations which claimed that they were simply responding to consumer preferences for their products.

Advertising as information is, like advertising, a partial truth. The classified sections of newspapers are witness to the important informational role of advertising. It may, in certain markets, be beneficial not to have bans on advertising. Price advertising may, under certain regulatory constraints, be a valuable source of information, but the information approach neglects the role of advertising in preference formation and much analysis is based on neo-classical models with little attention to advertising in oligopolistic markets and situations of monopolistic competition. The social structure of markets and its influence on preference formation is apparently ignored through the abstract conception of the utility-maximising consumer. Many policy prescriptions, as in the case of price advertising, are not based on abstract modelling, but on empirical guesses about consumer behaviour, which are likely to be heavily larded with value judgments, the very thing which the abstract model was intended to avoid. It has often been a form of ideological rather than scientific discourse. It has been an attractive discourse in the policy arena, particularly in relation to regulatory agencies, partly because it seems to legitimate outcomes in non-ideological terms. This appeals to decision makers whose authority is based on expertise rather than political representation.[42] But it is

[42] See D. Kennedy, "Distributive and Paternalist Motives in Contract and Tort Law, with Special Reference to Compulsory Terms and Unequal Bargaining Power" (1981–82) 41 *Maryland Law Review* 563 at 604.

often a curious mixture of analysis, armchair empiricism and social value judgments often prefaced by overbroad generalisations about the central role of advertising in a free market. It is one significant story about advertising but it is not the only show in town.

3 Preference Manipulation

The idea of the manipulable consumer is reflected in a number of legal doctrines such as the standard of the credulous consumer in relation to misleading advertising, and the doctrine of artificial product differentiation. The latter refers to the creation of illusory differences between products, sustained by image advertising. In addition, regulation of advertising which exploits consumer emotions, such as parental concern for the welfare of their children, may also fall within this category.

Although lawyers have not developed a coherent theory of advertising as preference manipulation, economists have long recognised that advertising may change tastes as well as provide information. The relatively thin theory of consumer behaviour evident in the neo-classical economic model of consumer sovereignty—that people choose what they prefer—has never completely dominated the literature. The conception of preferences as socially conditioned goes back at least to Veblen. In the 1920s, Chamberlin stressed the importance of selling costs in his theory of monopolistic competition. He argued that advertising might manipulate preferences through taste transfer:

"... selling methods which play upon the buyer's susceptibilities, which use against him the laws of psychology with which he is unfamiliar and therefore against which he cannot defend himself ... all of these have nothing to do with his knowledge. They are not informative; they are manipulative. They create a new scheme of wants".[43]

Galbraith's concept of the "dependence effect," where producers use advertising to create wants rather than respond to consumer needs, is probably the best known modern statement of the preference manipulation thesis in relation to those consumer markets dominated

---

[43] E. Chamberlin, *The Theory of Monopolistic Competition* (6th. ed., 1950), at 119–120.

by large corporations operating in oligopolistic markets. Galbraith argued that:

"The even more direct link between production and wants is provided by the institutions of modern advertising and salesmanship. These cannot be reconciled with the notion of independently determined desires, for their central function is to create desires—to bring into being wants that previously did not exist".[44]

Economic analysis has confronted directly the impact of advertising on taste and preference in the area of product differentiation and trademark law. Several questions are posed by the practice of brand advertising to differentiate products. First, to what extent can advertising create barriers to market entry and result in monopoly rents through artificial product differentiation? Secondly, is there a socially desirable level of product differentiation? Finally, to what extent does image and brand advertising result in irrational decision-making by consumers. Most economic analysis in this area has concentrated on the potential impact of product differentiation and brand image advertising on creating monopoly power, barriers to market entry and consequently elevated prices.[45] For example, the Federal Trade Commission in its action against breakfast cereal manufacturers argued that high advertising levels by the big three manufacturers contributed to the fact that there had been no new entrants to the industry between 1950 and 1972, notwithstanding the fact that it was a rapidly growing sector.[46] Although there might be no monopoly profits to any one firm the continuously high proliferation of advertised products created barriers to market entry.

Although there is evidence in some consumer markets of a statistically significant relationship between intensive image differentiation and monopoly profits, the issue remains contested. The currently dominant neo-classical framework has rejected the idea of the anti-competitive effects of advertising and brand images as barriers to entry. This is

---

[44] J. K. Galbraith, *The Affluent Society* (4th. ed., 1984), p. 129.
[45] See generally, F. Scherer, *Industrial Market Structure and Economic Performance* (2nd ed., 1980) pp. 386–405.
[46] For a valuable analysis of this and other cases of this period, see E. Mensch and A. Freeman, "Efficiency and Image: Advertising as an Antitrust Issue" (1990) *Duke L. J.* 321.

reflected in current fashions in antitrust where issues of product differentiation are sometimes regarded as the relic of the outdated hostility of economists to the role of advertising in the economy. In addition, it is argued that trademarks and associated images, like advertising, provide valuable information and lower search costs. The fact that a branded good may contain the same formula as an unbranded good "does not make them of equal quality to even the most coolly rational consumer. . . . [T]he consumer will be willing to pay a premium for greater assurance that the good will be manufactured to the specification of the formula . . . [T]rademarks enable the consumer to economize on a real cost because he spends less time searching to get the quality he wants."[47]

Arguments that consumers are being taken advantage of may always be met by the counter-argument that brand advertising provides information about a product and consumers may be willing to pay more for the assurance of brand quality or the status of the "right" beer. The economic study of this area is hampered by the difficulties of holding many variables constant (especially quality) and the lack of any clear norms as to the optimal level of product differentiation. It is very difficult for economists to make scientific statements about how much variety and differentiation there should be in the consumer marketplace.

Artificial product differentiation is in fact a challenge to neo-classical economics. If fully informed consumers buy a branded product which is identical in content to a non-branded product, at a higher price, then does this not result in "irrational consumer allegiances"[48] and raise questions about rational consumer choice? The remarkably broad protection afforded by trademark law to product images, suggests that these irrational consumer allegiances are important investments carefully nurtured by advertising.

Neo-classical economics assumes that changes in market behaviour are caused by changes in prices and income affecting the supply and demand of commodities. Stable preferences are an assumption of their analysis. If preferences are indeed moulded by the market or producers, as argued by Galbraith, then this undercuts the power of the model to

---

[47] W. Landes and R. Posner, "Trademark Law: An Economic Perspective" (1987) 30 *Journal of Law and Economics* 265 at 275.
[48] See Browning J. in *Smith v. Chanel* 402 F. 2d. 562 (1968) quoting from Panadreou, "The Economic Effects of Trademarks" (1956) 44 *California L. R.* 503 at 509.

predict behavioural change in terms of price change. Stigler and Becker in a famous article[49] attempt to defend neo-classical analysis and the assumption of stable preferences. They argue that consumers when purchasing goods or services are not merely purchasing the commodity, but are maximising their utility through the goods, which might include distinction and status. They recognise, therefore, the potentially symbolic nature of consumption and argue that the mix of consumption will relate to the relative cost of production of the particular good, such as distinction.

They argue that certain practices such as addictions, advertising, fashions and fads, which have been viewed as undermining the assumption of stable preferences, can be explained in terms of price theory. It is assumed that a person is attempting to maximise their utility through the particular use which they make of commodities depending on their time, skills, training and so on. Addictions (which appear to confound the law of diminishing marginal utility) are explained as the accumulation of consumption capital by consumers which increases the productivity of time spent in a beneficial addiction (such as listening to music) and the marginal utility of time allocated to listening to music. Harmful addictions are explained as a rise in the cost of production, for example, of pleasure from heroin. Advertising, according to Becker and Stigler, does not manipulate taste. In their model, consumers have imperfect information and producers may use advertising to differentiate their product. Consumers purchase the extra information attached to the product by paying higher prices. This is similar to the argument that consumers purchase branded goods for the extra information which is produced by the brand (*i.e.* reliable quality or status). Finally they argue that "fashions and fads" are explained by a demand for distinction or style which is the commodity produced by fashion. This demand will vary with social and economic environment. Since the ability to be distinct depends in part on the incomes of other consumers, they argue that as incomes rise in a society there will be greater expense incurred to achieve distinction from ones peers. Thus wealthy countries such as the USA will pay more attention to fashion than poor countries such as India.

Stigler and Becker's article is, in their own words, "an assertion" rather than a proposition of logic. They believe that it has greater

---

[49] G. Stigler and G. Becker, "*De Gustibus non est disputandum*" (1977) *American Econ. Rev.* 76.

power in predicting and explaining behaviour than explanations which refer to taste change. The proof would be in the empirical pudding. Unfortunately there is little empirical, as opposed to mathematical, testing of their propositions so that much of their analysis is based on armchair empirical observations such as that fashion is more significant in richer than poorer countries.

Their analysis indicates the recognition by economists that consumers are not simply buying a material commodity with an objective value, but that they are purchasing added value in terms of information or distinction. Consumption is as much an act of production where consumers add value to products by the use which they make of the goods which may be both symbolic and functional. At the same time the assumption that taste is stable across populations means that there is no need to investigate issues of taste formation or to complicate the predictive model with questions of taste change. Whatever consumers do in the market will be assumed to be utility-maximising in response to changes in prices and incomes and economists need not get into the messy questions of value judgments about the worth of preferences. If consumers buy images then they are simply optimising their utility. There is curiously one intriguing connection between Stigler, Becker and aspects of cultural studies. The argument that tastes do not vary suggests that there may be the possibility of a scientific study of taste in terms of its social role as cultural capital, a task undertaken by Bourdieu in his influential work *Distinction*.

Stigler and Becker attempt to avoid making value judgments, yet do not avoid drawing a distinction between good and bad addictions. Are there good or bad distinctions in relation to fashions or fads, for example? In their discussion of the role of advertising as information they argue that consumer utility from a product depends on "knowledge of its true *or alleged* properties" and that this knowledge whether "real or *fancied*" is produced by the advertising of products.[50] If the knowledge is fancied, for example, that there is a difference between particular brands, or in Mr Overton's case (above, p.16) that a particular brand of beer would make him attractive sexually, then what are we to say of the rationality of consumer choice and the nature of consumer preferences?

Other economists have investigated the role of advertising in relation

---

[50] See Mensch and Freeman *op. cit.*, p. 353 n. 134.

to the interdependence of utilities, recognising that an individual's welfare may depend on the consumption decisions of their peers.[51] Economists encounter difficulties in making a clear statement of the social welfare issues in situations where advertising exploits this interdependency. Perhaps the best known example is the frequent model changes in U.S. automobiles in the 1950s. Was this a positive contribution to social welfare? Scherer comments that:

"clearly, new car buyers pay more than if model changes were effected less often. Equally clearly, they freely elect to do so, for they have the option of holding on to their present auto longer or buying last year's model or an import restyled less frequently. By the stern criterion of consumer sovereignty, styling rivalry would seem to emerge with only minor scars. Still this is not completely convincing. The interdependence of consumer preferences complicates matters. Smith may buy a new model only because he fears that if he does not and neighbour Jones does, his utility will be reduced. Jones perceives the situation symmetrically, and both end up buying new models, though neither might if they could find some way to enforce mutual (and more widespread) buying restraint".[52]

The pervasiveness of advertising's exploitation of interdependent utilities, such as the importance of achieving the standard package of goods and services which usually exceeds significantly the statistical average, underlines the importance of thinking seriously about the possibility of the political process enforcing Scherer's "mutual buying restraint". It is as if consumers are caught in a classic prisoner's dilemma, where some mechanism for mutual co-operation might satisfy individual desires which are hampered by problems of collective co-ordination. At the least it also suggests that attention be paid to the potential costs of this form of advertising in contemporary societies. There is no room in the economic calculation for the potential alienation which such advertising causes to those who foresee little hope of

---

[51] Scherer argues that buying a product to keep up with trendsetters "can destroy utility along with creating it. To be sure, by responding to the stimulus and buying an advertised product, consumers may feel they are gaining something worthwhile. But it is not clear they have done any more than return to the satisfaction level they would have maintained without the persuasive assault on their preference structures." See *op. cit.*, at 381 n. 45.

[52] *ibid.*, at 398–99. See F. Fisher, Z. Grüiches & C. Kaysen, "The Costs of Automobile Model Changes Since 1949" (1962) 70 J. Pol. Econ. 433.

ever achieving the standard package. This is what economists would presumably view as an externality: the fact that television advertising makes advertising information available not only to potential consumers but also to individuals who are not in the market. Although many economists might agree with Scherer's concerns, they seem to be frozen in indecision when faced with suggesting policy prescriptions. They point to the potential futility of regulating this type of advertising, the difficulties of selecting the appropriate target, and the fear that government is unlikely to outperform the market in determining the optimal level of product differentiation.[53]

It is as if the scientific rhetoric of economics runs out at the end of every discussion of product differentiation and preference manipulation, so that we are left with the adage that the issue of the social costs of these advertising practices involves moral judgments over which reasonable persons may disagree.[54]

The economic work on advertising and product differentiation suggests, therefore, the need for further probing of the sources of consumer taste and preferences. Recent progressive-liberal work[55] has challenged both the thin theory of consumer sovereignty in the economic literature and the conception of politics as following private preferences. The challenge draws on psychological and economic work on the limits of consumer rationality which suggest that consumers do not act in the manner of the neoclassical model, and which proposes a conception of politics as the opportunity for the moulding and transformation of preferences: an opportunity for the "public and rational discussion about the common good."[56] Citizens may wish, like Ulysses, to foreclose

---

[53] See Scherer, *op. cit.*, at 404 n. 45.

[54] *ibid.*, at 380.

[55] I am thinking particularly of articles such as C. Sunstein, "Legal Interference with Private Preferences" (1986) 53 U. Chi. L. Rev. 1129 and his text *After the Rights Revolution: Reconceiving the Regulatory State* (1990). These works provide a useful source of references in psychology, economics, and political theory which furnish the basis for critiquing the thin theory of private preferences in neo-classical economics.

[56] "Much more important ... is the idea that the central concern of politics should be the *transformation of preferences* rather than their aggregation. On this view the core of the political process is the public and rational discussion about the common good, not the isolated act of voting according to private preferences ... [politics involves] purging the private, selfish or idiosyncratic preferences in open and public debate." See J. Elster, *Sour Grapes: Studies in the Subversion of Rationality* (1983), p. 35. Owen Fiss has articulated a similar model as a normative basis for adjudication. See O. Fiss, "The Forms of Justice" (1979) 93 Harv. L. R. 1.

or restrict future choices which as consumers they might succumb to.[57] Welfare economics recognises this distinction between the citizen and the consumer. Musgrave wrote that:

> "the individual voter dealing with political issues has a frame of reference quite distinct from that which underlies his allocation of income as a consumer. In the latter situation the voter acts as a private individual determined by self interest and deals with his personal wants; in the former, he acts as a political being guided by his image of a good society."[58]

It is also pointed out that existing market preferences are a function of current legal rules and social conditions and are, therefore, shifting and not static. They are social constructions. There is, therefore, no such thing as social or legal institutions simply following preferences. To do so is to make a conscious choice of endorsing a particular set of preferences.[59] An important concept in this literature is that of "adaptive preferences". Individuals may adapt their preferences to the particular social choices and opportunities available. It is, therefore, inappropriate to take these preferences as necessarily justifying the status quo. Recognition of these arguments reduces objections to public measures which attempt to change preferences in order to achieve greater social welfare or individual autonomy. For example, many consumers may have adapted their behaviour to the structure of automobile selling with its cultural rituals of negotiation. It is not clear that this must be assumed to be what they would ideally prefer as the market form.

The main bite of this progressive critique is the attempt to change the terms of debate over government regulation, problematising simple conceptions of paternalism and consumer sovereignty and arguing that many regulatory programmes which appear to interfere with consumer

---

[57] See J. Elster, *Ulysses and the Sirens: Studies in Rationality and Irrationality* (1979). Examples might include door-to-door sales, seat belts, the use of hazardous products, and controls on life style advertising. Public broadcasting might be justified as dealing with the situation where the short term costs of appreciating this type of broadcasting are high, but the long term benefits are higher.

[58] R. Musgrave, *The Theory of Public Finance*, (1959), pp. 87–88.

[59] Neatly put by Bernard Williams in his critique of utilitarianism: "To engage in those processes which utilitarianism regards as just 'following' is ... itself doing something: it is choosing to endorse those preferences, or some set of them, which lie on the surface, as determined by such things as what people at a given moment regard as possible—something which in its turn is affected by the activities of government." See J. Smart & B. Williams, *Utilitarianism For and Against* (1979), pp. 147–48.

preferences, in fact, promote values of autonomy and social welfare
and reflect democratic desires. It also reiterates the point made by
realist writers, such as Hale[60] and Dawson,[61] that the market is not a
natural prepolitical institution and that the particular form of market
relations reflects a political compromise backed up by state force. Issues
of consumer protection, such as control of advertising, may be viewed,
therefore, as establishing and changing ground rules, rather than as
"intervention" in a private sphere or paternalistically overruling individual preferences.

This modified preference formation approach also leads to some
reflections on structure and agency in modern life. We seem, within
this approach, to be multiple selves[62] depending on the institutional
context. The social constructionism of sociology challenges the agency
of liberal philosophy. This work promises to go beyond the simple
dichotomies of the rational or manipulated consumer. Its limitation is
that it has not thus far examined carefully these issues of structure and
agency within the context of the cultural forces which have historically
shaped the modern consumer society.

Summary

These three narratives exhaust law's truth concerning the power of
advertising over consumer behaviour. In both advertising as information
and advertising as manipulation there is often a common assumption
concerning the power of advertising and the relationship between
power and knowledge. Power is generally conceived as power *over*
economic choices in the market and it is assumed that this power is

---

[60] R. Hale, "Coercion and Distribution in A Supposedly Non Coercive State" (1923) 38
Pol. Sci. L. Q. 470 and "Bargaining, Duress and Economic Liberty" (1943) 43 Colum.
L. R. 603.
[61] "The system of 'free' contract described by nineteenth-century theory is now coming
to be recognized as a world of fantasy, too orderly, too neatly contrived, and too
harmonious to correspond with reality. As welcome fiction is slowly displaced by sober
fact, the regime of 'freedom' can be visualized as merely another system, more elaborate
and more highly organized, for the exercise of economic pressure." See J. Dawson,
"Economic Duress and the Fair Exchange in French and German Law" (1937) 11
Tul. L. Rev. 345.
[62] See the discussion in D. Parfit, *Reasons and Persons* (1984).

measurable in empirical terms. Economic theory and positivistic social science would test the validity of arguments about the power of advertising. Policy documents and academic writing continue to advocate the greater use of social science expertise in advertising regulation. The example of artificial product differentiation showed the limits of this approach. It indicated the potential value of understanding the cultural role of brand and image advertising and the cultural shaping of individual choice.

There is a conflict between the vision of advertising as a contribution to rational choice and advertising as manipulation. The manipulation thesis may reflect at times a deeper vision of markets. The metaphor of seduction which is often associated with manipulation[63] evokes a vision of consumer markets as sites of sensual and erotic gratification, contrasting historically with the supposed manly values of productivism.[64] Consumption markets, while promoting self-transformation, involved a potential loss of self-control. This critique is open to the argument that critics "harbor puritanical traits: a distrust of fantasy and sensuous display, a preference for production over consumption, a manipulative model of advertising as social control and a masculine bias that led them to typecast the mass of consumers as passive and feminine".[65]

There are clearly dangers in the manipulation argument slipping into simple apolitical moralisms as a substitute for a serious critique of the cultural significance and power of advertising.

The rational/manipulation dichotomy apparent in legal analysis also reflects views on structure and agency in social life. The law seems to view the consumer either as a puppet of false consciousness or a rational subject making careful choices. Decisions about whether individuals are manipulated tend to be made on the basis of judicial "common sense". This common sense which assumes in general an autonomous legal subject has been challenged by writers who have indicated that individuals' market preferences are shaped by legal rules and social norms. In the next chapter we shall develop this idea in the concept of the socially situated subject, with a focus on how individuals constitute themselves as consumers, through repeated market activity where individuals are invited continually to "buy in" to the role of consumer.

---

[63] See above, Chap. 1, nn. 18 and 20.
[64] See J. Lears, *Fables of Abundance* (1995), p. 4.
[65] *ibid.*, p. 4.

Feminist theory has also critiqued the legal model of the subject as coherent, rational and autonomous and has drawn attention to the social discipline of everyday practices concerning dress and the body, a staple of advertising, and the oppressive power of these norms. The development of the "battered woman's defence"[66] to prosecutions for murder of an intimate partner recognises the shaping effect of social and cultural practices. The concept of power which emerges in these forms of analysis is, therefore, more complex than the dichotomy of rationality/manipulation and suggests that this shaping of consciousness is not simply a phenomenon of social control by powerful economic actors.

The common sense of consumerism supports the continued production of new consumption as a necessary aspect of the accumulation of capital, but it is a common sense which also needs to continually reproduce the subject of the market—the consumer. This requires not merely "the production of new needs"[67] but a subject with particular dispositions towards the consumption process. The next chapter explores the constitution of this consumer subject and the role of discourses such as advertising in this process, set against the background of the institutional framework of consumer capitalism.

---

[66] See *R. v. Lavellee* (1990) 55 C.C.C. (3d) 97 (S.C.C.).
[67] K. Marx, *Grundrisse* (1973) p. 408 quoted in D. Harvey, *The Limits to Capital* (1982), p. 8.

Chapter 3

Culture, Power and Advertising

Erik Barnouw's excellent history of the U.S. television industry describes the rise after the Second World War of a "consciousness industry", which promoted consumption of products as the answer to every problem: "[p]roducts seemed the key to success in business, romance, community status and the well being of the nation. Problems ranging from headaches to loneliness to obesity to personal failure to dangerous addictions were solved by products."[1] The dominance of this "consciousness industry" in social economic and cultural life is a central feature of contemporary consumer capitalism. Advertising, promotion and market research (consumer marketing) is now a global industry, producing a vast private sociology of consumer behaviour and motivation that is deployed in the search for ever-increasing sales.[2]

Psychological marketing, branding and image marketing are basic elements of the promotion of goods and services. Advertising and marketing link the economic market to culture by associating products

---

[1] E. Barnouw, *Tube of Plenty* (2nd. ed.) (1990), p. 540.

[2] For historical explorations of the development of these aspects of consumer capitalism see S. Strasser, *Satisfaction Guaranteed: The Making of the American Mass Market* (1989); J. Lears, *Fables of Abundance: A Cultural History of Advertising in America* (1994); S. Ewen, *Captains of Consciousness* (1976); A. Wernick, *Promotional Culture* (1992); W. Leiss, S. Kline and S. Jhally, *Social Communication in Advertising* (2nd. ed., 1990); for an analysis of the nature of changes in corporate structure, A. Chandler, *The Visible Hand: The Managerial Revolution in American Business* (1977). The idea of a "private sociology" of consumer behaviour is taken from W. M. O'Barr, *Culture and the Ad: Exploring Otherness in the World of Advertising* (1994), p. 201. The relationship of information technology to the development of sophisticated marketing is explored in O. Gandy Jr., *The Panoptic Sort: A Political Economy of Personal Information* (1993). For an excellent analysis of the changes in marketing and the attempt by manufacturers to harness the law of property to manufacturer-dominated markets see Z. Chafee, "Equitable Servitudes on Chattels" (1928) Harv. L. R. 945 at 947.

with a wide variety of individual and social values. The harnessing of the electronic media to commercial interests, achieved at an early date in the USA, where broadcasters sell audiences to advertisers, has intensified the spread of this consumer culture.

The massive upsurge of academic writing on the culture of consumerism has often drawn distinctions between differing phases in the development of consumer capitalism. The post second world war economic system, sometimes described as Fordism,[3] promised the benefits of the consumer society for members of the working-classes (those headed by white males) in unionised employment. Full employment with guaranteed collective bargaining rights ensured high wages which could finance through consumer credit the purchase of the commodities manufactured by the productive system. This consumer culture was exported during this period though the dominance of U.S. media production, and the dominance of the U.S. in the international non-communist economies.

Since the early 1970s writers have attempted to describe a new system of capitalism which is emerging, a task spurred in recent years by the demise of state communist systems.[4] A central argument is that countries of the North have experienced an increasing penetration of commercialised relations throughout all levels of private life, including the family, leisure activities and sexual relations. Just as capitalist forms of exchange had slowly colonised the world of work, so the field of consumption was becoming increasingly colonised. The culture of consumerism, interweaving cultural signs of distinction and personal achievement with commodities, insinuated all parts of society through the electronic media. Indeed, the forms of advertising and promotion seemed to have become primary forms of social communication. For example, ideas are "sold" or "packaged". Individuals learn to promote their "image". Consumerism is an important cultural aspect of the

---

[3] See discussion of fordism in M. Piore and C. Sabel, *The Second Industrial Divide* (1984). There remains controversy as to the nature of fordism and its continued existence. Aronowitz argues that the key features of fordism were "the development of consumer credit, a floor under consumption through the provision of state pensions, unemployment benefits and other income transfers" S. Aronowitz, *The Politics of Identity—Class Culture, Social Movements* (1992), p. 7.

[4] Important works here are A. Touraine, *The Post-Industrial Society* (1972); F. Jameson *Post Modernism, or the Cultural Logic of Late Capitalism* (1991); D. Harvey, *The Condition of PostModernity: An Enquiry into the Nature of Cultural Change* (1989).

contemporary multifaceted phenomenon of globalisation.[5]

The extension of commodity relations beyond work and into all areas of social life increasingly politicises areas traditionally regarded as part of the private realm. In Fordism the main terrain of social conflict was the workplace. For moderate reformers the issue was the division of profits between labour and capital and control of working conditions. Within critical theory the working class remained the engine of social change. In contrast, in post-fordism writers draw attention to the many social movements associated with consumption relations, such as environmentalism, urban politics[6] (concerning the balance of collective and private consumption) and feminism.[7] These movements undermined traditional distinctions between the public and private sphere. They also problematised distinctions between production and consumption. Feminist analysis undermined the concept of the family as a site of private consumption, highlighting the important role of women as unpaid home labourers and as reproducers of labour power. Women's inequality was a complex amalgam of structures of oppression in the private and public sphere.

The spread of the ideology of consumerism has also had a radical impact in challenging traditional forms of authority. Parents seem to lose control over consumer-conscious kids, as commercial lifestyles permeate childhood. The authority of "high culture" as a critique of consumerism is undermined as it is increasingly enmeshed in popular culture. A different style of politics is also discernible. Issues of autonomy and identity compete with the traditional Fordist question of the redistribution of resources.[8] One writer has suggested that cultural domination rather than material inequality has become the main form

---

[5] I have not attempted to theorise this phenomenon. De Sousa Santos refers to globalisation as "a multifaceted phenomenon with economic, social, political, cultural, religious and legal dimensions intertwined in most complex ways." De Sousa Santos, *op. cit.*, p. 253.

[6] See M. Castells, *The Urban Question: A Marxist Approach* (1977), *The Informational City* (1989); P. Saunders, *Social Class and Stratification* (1990). See also C. Stanley, "Repression and Resistance: Problems of Regulation in contemporary Urban Culture, Parts and II" (1993) 21 *International Journal of the Sociology of Law* 23 and 121.

[7] See E. Laclau and C. Mouffe, *Hegemony and Socialist Strategy: Towards a Radical Democratic Politics* (1985).

[8] See the discussion of this in C. Offe, "Challenging the Boundaries of Institutional Politics: Social Movements since the 1960s" in *Changing Boundaries of the Political* (C. Maier ed., 1987), chap. 2.

of political mobilisation in this society.[9] In addition, the potentially radical slogans which accompanied the promotion of consumerism, such as "freedom of choice" and the equation of democracy and empowerment with the ownership of goods, could be turned into a critique of the real inequalities in a society based on private consumption.[10]

In the introductory chapter I suggested that there were contrasting views of consumerism as alienation and consumerism as empowerment. Within theories of the development of consumer capitalism there is a relatively long tradition of viewing consumerism as alienation, a form of false consciousness, where a democracy of goods substituted for true democratic citizenship. The distinction between true and false needs was emphasised by Herbert Marcuse who argued that "most of the prevailing needs to relax, to have fun, to behave and consume in accordance with the advertisements, to love and hate what others love and hate, belong to this category of false needs".[11] True needs were those uninfluenced by the distorting social and cultural arrangements of monopoly capitalism. Commodity consumption substituted for loss of control by large numbers of individuals over their conditions of labour while advertising contributed an important role to a growing corporate authoritarianism by maintaining a consumption-based cultural stability and defusing the potential for class conflict.[12]

More recent writing in a number of genres has drawn a more complex picture. In particular, they have criticised the idea that there is an "authentic self", which would appear in the absence of the alienating effects of consumer culture. The subject of consumer society is a social construction, a product of social practices and discourses. Recognising that we are socially situated subjects, much attention has focused on how discourses, such as media and advertising, may shape subjectivities and the extent to which individuals construct identities from the slogans of popular culture. Frank Mort argues, for example, that in contemporary consumer cultures "there is a proliferation of individualities on offer" ... and "post-modern structures of identity are

---

[9] N. Fraser "From Redistribution to Recognition? Dilemmas of Justice in a 'Post-Socialist' Age" (1996) *New Left Review* 68.
[10] "Interpellated as equals in their capacity as consumers, ever more groups are impelled to reject the real inequalities which continue to exist". Laclau and Mouffe, *op. cit.*, p. 164.
[11] H. Marcuse, *One Dimensional Man* (1964), p. 5.
[12] This was the argument made by Ewen, *op. cit.*, n.2.

less centred around the certainty of a fixed self. We do not often get the reassurance of a coherent subjectivity these days politically or culturally."[13]

To some the fluidity of the self offers the possibility for resistance to domination or the opportunity to "mess with" and subvert traditional images and roles such as those of gender. Exploration and exploitation of such possibilities are major themes within the post-modern politics of identity in consumption relations.

An uneasy tension between alienation and empowerment figures significantly in much contemporary work on consumption relations. Mica Nava, for example, drawing on the analysis of Foucault, argues that although consumerism reinforced the subordination of women in the post-war era, the social emphasis on consumption as opposed to production provided an important source of power for women. It served as a source for the politicisation of white middle-class women and drew attention to the relatively subordinate role of women outside the home.[14]

Ideas about the power of advertising have tracked these general themes. The conception of advertising as social control[15] has been modified to view it as an important source of ideological meanings in society which invite individuals to reproduce the culture of consumption by "buying in" to the stories in the advertisements.[16] In turn, this approach has been challenged by arguments which attribute greater agency to the audiences of advertisements who may subvert the preferred meanings of the texts to their own ends. The assumptions and analysis of these theories concerning the power of advertising have significant implications for legal assumptions about the power of advertising and the ability to regulate this power.

These initial commentaries on consumer capitalism suggest that an important issue is the relationship between consumerism as a general social ideology and the ways in which this culture is inscribed in the details of individual behaviour, as consumer culture is produced,

---

[13] F. Mort, "The Politics of Consumption" in *New Times: The Changing Face of Politics in the 1990s* (S. Hall and M. Jacques ed., 1989), 169.

[14] M. Nava, "Consumerism and its Contradictions" (1987) 1.2 *Cultural Studies* 204.

[15] See, *e.g.* D. Potter, *People of Plenty: Economic Abundance and the American Character* (1958) where it is argued at p. 166 that advertising was "really one of the very limited group of institutions which exercise social control".

[16] See J. Williamson, *Decoding Advertisements: Ideology and Meaning in Advertisements* (1978) and see more extended discussion below.

reproduced or challenged in everyday life. Consumer markets are not only economic institutions where there might be economic imbalance between producers and consumers. They are also important sites for the establishment and challenging of identities, for contests over the representation of social groups and the social relations of consumption. A major challenge for scholars is to understand the relationship between the routine of daily life and the reproduction of social ideologies of consumerism.

1 Power, Domination and Everyday Life: Cultural Studies

Advertising representations and images are a routine part of life in consumer capitalism. They have a "taken for granted" character. The field of cultural studies[17] focuses on the everyday world of consumption practices, leisure and entertainment and the relationship between these practices and the reproduction of social relations of domination. What role do practices such as "listening to the radio, watching television, going to see films, experiencing music, going shopping, reading magazines and newspapers and participating in ... other forms of media culture"[18] play in inducing individuals to accept or question the existing organisation of power in society? An initial response to this question may be found in theories about the role of ideology in securing assent in society.

Cultural studies owes much to the work of Antonio Gramsci who described the role of mainstream culture in a society as providing a hegemonic world view, a common sense which rationalised the interests of the minority in power as representing the interests of society as a whole.[19] Within Marxist theory Gramsci focused on the importance of this ideological struggle over meaning, arguing that ideological issues could not simply be read off as mere superstructure on economic

---

[17] See App. 1 on cultural studies.
[18] D. Kellner, *Media Culture* (1995) quoted in K. Thompson, *Key Quotations in Sociology* (1996), p. 72.
[19] An excellent essay which discusses Gramsci among others in the context of the development of cultural studies is S. Hall, "The Problem of Ideology: Marxism without Guarantees" (1986) *Journal of Communication Inquiry* 10(2) 28.

relations. Hegemony was not imposed by fiat of the dominant interests of capital, but operated through many differing institutions in society. It required the intellectual and moral leadership of the professional and managerial classes and intellectuals and others who helped to shape the bounds of conventional wisdom. He stressed both the importance of this common sense in societies and also the fact that it was a site of ideological struggle. Ideas about democracy in capitalist societies would take on a common sense understanding which reflected bourgeois conceptions of democracy but there was the possibility of challenging this conception, based on older or more utopian conceptions of democracy.

Gramsci suggested that the study of social power involved a broad study of the lived culture of a society which included the "whole way of life"[20] of a society. Within the media-dominated culture of modern consumer capitalism it is necessary to understand how the discourses of advertising and the media may be more or less effective in circulating particular images and representations, preferring certain social meanings and in normalising particular forms of social domination. The idea of power in this style of analysis is more complex than conceptions of legal power over an individual or economic power which may limit choices in the market. Cultural power does not reside in an identifiable institution but is rather something which circulates throughout private and social relations.[21] This form of power shapes an individual's sense of who they are and their relationships with others. In this sense it is a constitutive power. A media which continually represents individuals as consumers helps to constitute individuals as consumers. The intersection of economy and culture in the consumer marketplace means that there is a convergence of economic and cultural power. Liberal conceptions of the individual and approaches to markets based on liberal individualism, such as law and economics, neglect cultural conceptions of power. They assume the model of the free-standing subject with a unified identity acting upon the external world. Cultural studies posits the idea of socially situated subjects who are partly a product of existing social relations and who are continually constituting and reconstituting themselves through existing linguistic and cultural codes. The sharp distinction between structure and agency is problematised in this work.

---

[20] R. Williams, *Culture and Society* (1963), p. 273.
[21] This idea of power is identified with the work of Foucault. See M. Foucault, *op. cit.*, p. 132.

There is a large literature in cultural studies. In order to illustrate themes of relevance to this study I have chosen three topics: cultural analyses of how advertising works to prefer meanings and the role of the consumer in reading the images and texts of advertising; feminist approaches to consumer culture, advertising and representations of women in popular culture; Bourdieu's analysis of class and culture and the role of culture as marking class distinctions and as a site for class conflict.

2 Reading Advertisements Culturally

One of the most interesting questions about the power of advertising is the simple question of how individual advertisements actually work to prefer certain meanings and reproduce particular social ideologies. This issue is of great significance because it links the everyday world which we experience as consumers to larger questions about the reproduction of particular forms of life which may sustain inequality and domination in society. One of the best starting points is the work of Judith Williamson[22] who illustrates how advertisements do not impose their meaning upon us from above but that we actively construct the meaning of an advertisement, at the same time reproducing dominant norms. Advertising generally works by drawing connections between the signifier (the object) and the signified (*e.g.* beauty, erotic satisfaction). For example, a picture of Catherine Deneuve beside Chanel No. 5 invites an individual to see the product in terms of glamour and beauty, substituting the product for both Catherine Deneuve and what she signifies. Distinctions in social symbols are used to create distinctions between products. Consumer objects do not have a fixed meaning but are connected and reconnected by advertising with different cultural signs. The image of Marlboro cigarettes was originally that of female elegance. It was only in 1955 that the Marlboro cowboy rode onto the scene to change the image. Products are often "floating signifiers". They do not have a fixed identity and much consumption is the consumption of signs which create distinctions between consumption groups.

---

[22] J. Williamson, *Decoding Advertisements: Ideology and Meaning in Advertising* (1984).

A central point in Williamson's analysis is that knowledge of the connections in the advertisement is not intrinsic to the advertisements. Consumers actively construct the meaning through reading the advertisement. Advertising leaves not only spaces to fill with meaning but also spaces to position the reader. Reading an advertisement is not the same as viewing a conventional painting. In the latter situation the viewer is essentially a spectator. With an advertisement the reader may be invited to occupy an imaginary space in the advertisement, which often has significant class, gender and racial overtones. An advertisement may be designed to exclude particular viewers from seeing themselves in the advertisement through the use of models of a particular race or age. The bottom line in almost all advertisements is to view the signified (attractiveness, democracy, peace of mind) in terms of an object which can be purchased. By continually repeating this activity individuals are constructing themselves as consumers, reading into the advertisement the role of consumer. It is as if the advertisement shouts "hey you" and those identified immediately identify themselves within the advertisement.[23] To the extent that a person automatically "buys in" to these images and subject positions s/he may often be actively reproducing dominant ideologies within the advertisements, and reinforcing particular aspects of their own subjectivity. All of this interpretive work is done almost instantly so that it is thought to be natural or common sense to view the advertisement in this manner.

The power of discourses to affect individuals' conception of themselves and relationship to others is illustrated by Edward Said in his book *Orientalism* where he drew attention to the power of the Western discourse of Orientalism in constructing authoritative forms of knowledge about the Orient which were acted upon by researchers, politicians and administrators. These images were simply constructions which had little basis in reality. As Said states: "at most the 'real' Orient provoked a writer to his vision: it very rarely guided it".[24] Orientalism was a complex system of representation of "the other" and her/his difference from the West which Said traces through literary, anthropological, political and sociological discourses about the Orient.

---

[23] This is known as "interpellation" and owes its origins to the work of Althusser. A useful example of this positioning theory may be found in B. Bonney and H. Wilson, "Advertising and the Manufacture of Difference" in *The Media Reader* (M. Alvarado and J.O. Thompson ed., 1990), p. 181.

[24] E. Said, *Orientalism* (1979), p. 22.

These disciplines developed systematic constructions which provided an authoritative system of knowledge for making cultural comparison, moral judgments and sustaining colonial power. Said did not see this Orientalism as a simple reflection of economic power but nevertheless as a complex common sense which sustained differing forms of domination, including cultural domination. The image of "the other" sustained particular Western conceptions of culture and rationality which could be contrasted with the irrationality of the Orient. The construction of "the other" is never an innocent task since it will always have practical implications in terms of the exercise of power, whether that be imperialism, the exercise of immigration policy or the construction of the enemy. As Said argues "[T]he construction of identity is bound up with the disposition of power and powerlessness in each society, and is therefore anything but mere academic woolgathering".[25] He also emphasises the contemporary importance of the electronic media, which is dominated by U.S. organisations, in intensifying cultural stereotypes drawn from Orientalism, and which marginalises alternative stories about U.S. relations with other countries.

An imaginative analysis of the power of ads which develops the above arguments may be found in O'Barr's *Culture and the Ad*.[26] O'Barr examined the structure and content of U.S. travel advertisements in 1929 and the late 1980s, and their construction of foreigners. He found remarkable continuity between the two eras. Rarely were social relationships between the Americans and foreigners depicted in an egalitarian manner. Americans were generally depicted in a superior role: the third world was often depicted as feminine and submissive and there was no direct interaction between the tourist and "the natives". These images, therefore, provided paradigms for relations between the intended audience (the tourist) and foreigners. O'Barr then analysed travel photographs which indicated what tourists saw as significant in their travels and their relationship to the countries visited. He found that these photographs often mirrored the patterns of advertisements, in particular the hierarchical relationship between tourist and native. The central point was that the advertising images were acted upon and practice was influenced by representation.

O'Barr provides concrete illustrations of Said's thesis in examples

---

[25] *ibid.*, p. 322.
[26] W.M. O'Barr, *Culture and the Ad: Exploring Otherness in the World of Advertising* (1994).

such as the portrayal of "the threat from abroad" in an advertisement for energy awareness which depicts an Arab holding Uncle Sam hostage. Said's argument is not restricted to depiction of the Orient but to all constructions through literature and popular texts of "the other" by dominant cultures. Women and minorities have often been constructed as "the other". Passivity, emotionalism and nurturing have been constructed as supposed feminine virtues to be contrasted with the supposed objectivity, rationality, and neutrality of white masculinity. Such constructions which claim to identify the essence of the other are not only about the exercise of power, but deny the complexity and richness of culture.[27]

These analyses indicate that the argument that advertising simply reflects society is inadequate. Advertising constructs representations of the social world, often from a limited set of categories drawn from market research and psychological profiles. This form of knowledge of society is then reproduced daily through advertisements. Consumers are not passive dupes but we may actively reproduce dominant images of social relations, constructing ourselves and others from representations in advertising and other social discourse. The common sense of advertising is part of a larger common sense such as the idea that consumerism allows us to escape from class distinctions and live in imagined communities of boomers, yuppies and so on. By identifying with what we consume, the real structures of social relations in society are obscured.

Although Williamson indicates an active role for the consumer, there seems little role for the consumer resisting the preferred meaning in the advertising text. Further analysis in cultural studies has argued that there may be greater possibility for consumers subverting the preferred meanings in texts. This is partly since advertisements may have to appeal to a broad audience and texts become polysemic, *i.e.* subject to many different interpretations. This recognition of the power of the audience to subvert the preferred meaning in the text was a reaction to earlier analysis that had recognised little agency for consumers. The argument developed, therefore, that popular culture, including advertising, might become the site for oppositional discourse to the dominant norms of consumer capitalism.

David Morley showed that different groups did not read the preferred

---

[27] See E. Said, *op. cit.*, p. 333 and see generally E. Said, *Culture and Imperialism* (1993).

meanings in television programmes but used them as the opportunity for developing oppositional readings.[28] Children seemed to use television programmes as a source of subversion to adult values and constructed their own set of values from the programmes.[29] Hebdige argued that American images in popular culture of the 1950s provided working class teenagers with the source of an oppositional identity to the anodyne characterisation of popular working-class culture on the BBC and other establishment media.[30] The existence of graffiti campaigns by feminists and others seemed to confirm the argument that where there was power there was resistance and it might be possible to steal elements of the dominant culture and use it against itself. This idea influenced the post-modern vision of the consumer as a subversive *bricoleur* building shifting identities from various cultural signs, never being caught in the freeze frame of a defined identity and therefore always in a state of potential liberation. This rather upbeat vision of popular culture has been critiqued as merely the musings of "left wing academics ... picking out strands of subversion in every piece of pop culture from street style to soap opera".[31] The politics of style is mistaken for a politics of substance.

To what extent is this idea of oppositional discourse apparent in advertising? One of the recent developments in advertising has been a change in advertising style. Advertisements present ambiguous images with apparently uncertain meaning compared with the Chanel No. 5 advertisement described above. It is sometimes difficult to determine whether something is an advertisement and what the connection is between the image and the product. There may be no product in the advertisement and Robert Goldman refers to this as the "this is not an ad-ad".[32] Advertisements show disjointed images ending with phrases such as "Just do it". This turns out to be an advertisement for trainers.

An extreme disjuncture between image and product appears in Benetton advertising where pictures of new-born babies, and AIDS victims are portrayed with the Benetton logo. The consumer is puzzled. What is the relationship between the product and the image? There

[28] See D. Morley, *Family Television: Cultural Power and Domestic Leisure* (1986).

[29] See B. Hodge and D. Tripp, *Children and Television: A Semiotic Approach* (1986). See also E. Seiter, *Sold Separately: Parents and Children in Consumer Culture* (1995).

[30] See D. Hebdige, *Hiding in the light* (1989).

[31] J. Williamson as quoted in M. Morris, "Banality in Cultural Studies" (1988) 10:2 *Discourse* 3.

[32] R. Goldman, *Reading Ads Socially* (1992), Chap. 7.

does not seem to exist the simple closure of the Chanel No. 5 advertisement where one almost automatically makes a connection between the image associated with Catherine Deneuve and Chanel No. 5. It is as if advertisers are opening up a space for the reflective consumer. But these new developments are an extension of product differentiation. The harder one works to understand the connections in the advertisement, the more one is likely to remember the image and the product. Moreover, the Benetton advertisement turns iconoclasm into a commodity.[33] Benetton executives argue that those who criticise their advertising are hypocritical since they do not complain about the emaciated white models in much everyday advertising and Benetton is simply injecting some real life into the make-believe world of advertising. This may also, of course, appeal to the younger cynical consumers who are targets for their products. Post-modernism celebrates iconoclasm, irony and parody but there is no reason to assume that these techniques are immune to commodification or that they are always on the side of the angels.[34]

3 Feminism, Foucault and Cultural Studies

Responsibility for and management of household consumption decisions has traditionally been women's sphere but this has often been overlooked in much consumer law and policy so that the impact of the consumer society on women has often been neglected.[35] Indeed one factor in the

---

[33] I found the following essay useful on this topic, N. Lisus, "Benetton's Post Modern Approach to A Humanist Ad: the evolution of a two-tiered text" unpublished paper, University of Toronto, Centre of Criminology, 1994.

[34] "Textuality, ambiguity, indeterminacy lie often enough on the side of dominant ideological discourses themselves." T. Eagleton, *Ideology* (1991), p. 198.

[35] See now, *e.g.* M. Luxton and H. Rosenberg, *op. cit.*, Chap. 2, n. 39, E. Seiter, *Sold Separately: Parents and Children in Consumer Culture* (1995), pp. 12–26, D. Hayden, *Redesigning the American Dream: The Future of Housing, Work and Family Life* (1984) "Special Issue: Gender and Consumer Policy" *Journal of Consumer Policy* (1995) and C. Wright, "Feminine Trifles of Vast Importance: Writing Gender into the History of Consumption" in *Gender Conflicts: New Essays in Women's History* F. Iacovetta and M. Valverde, eds., 1992, p. 229. The early development of white middle-class feminism in the USA stressed connections between everyday practices such as housework, fashion and standards of beauty and cultural oppression. In *The Female Mystique* (1963) Betty Friedan exposed the oppressive form of life which many white middle-class women lived in suburbia. This was not simply an economic form of oppression. In Rowbotham's words

dominance of the organisation of production as the explanatory variable in social theory may be related to a conception of consumption as women's sphere. The image of much consumption as supposedly irrational/feminine is evident in both social and legal discourse,[36] underlining a general tendency in many academic disciplines to regard women "as unpredictable bodies rather than rational beings".[37]

Both the work of Foucault and feminist analysis have recast thinking about the role of power in social life and the constitutive power of everyday practices, representations and normalising discourses in shaping individuals' conceptions of themselves and others and producing relations of subordination. The concept of power which emerges is more complex than the legal dichotomy of rationality/manipulation which we encountered in Chapter 1. The focus here is on the theme of cultural domination; the relationship between everyday representations and practices and the oppression of women.

One aspect of feminism has focused on the female body as a site of control and resistance, analysing such issues as beauty practices and their relationship to women's oppression.[38] Foucault described the body as an important site for disciplinary control, "the place in which the most minute and local social practices are linked up with the large scale organisation of power",[39] but feminists had long argued the connections between the social discipline in everyday practices of dress and body practices, and the production of ideals of femininity and social oppression. Mary Wollstonecraft lamented that "genteel women are, literally speaking, slaves to their bodies".[40]

The normalising power of fashion and body practices operates through individual self-regulation which is nonetheless connected to

---

"they did not lack for objects ... but somehow they felt that their lives were empty." (above, p. 9) Friedan described how marketing and advertising contributed to the idea of the "happy housewife" role quoting an advertising executive who stated: "Properly manipulated ... American housewives can be given the sense of identity, purpose, creativity, the self-realization, even the sexual joy they lack – by the buying of things." ibid., at 208.

[36] See discussion in J. Lears, *Fables of Abundance op. cit.*, Chap. 2, n. 18 and see below, Chap. 4.

[37] C. Smart *Feminism and the Power of Law* (1989) p. 91.

[38] Much of the following relies on the work of Susan Bordo. See S. Bordo, *Unbearable Weight: Feminism, Western Culture, and the Body* (1993).

[39] H. Dreyfus and P. Rabinow *Michel Foucault: Beyond Structuralism and Hermeneutics* (2nd ed., 1982), p. xxvi.

[40] Mary Wollstonecraft, *A Vindication of the Rights of Women* quoted in Bordo *op. cit.*, p. 18.

larger power relations. The idea of the "self-regulating subject" is reflected in the concept of the male gaze: "Men look at Women. Women watch themselves being looked at. This determines not only most relations between men and women, but also the relation of women to themselves".[41]

This conception of individual self-surveillance through the internalisation of the male gaze is of great importance in understanding the power of advertising. It is not necessary for women to accept the patriarchal subordination implicit in this gaze, but simply to adjust their behaviour to conform. As Cooper argues by reference to Foucault:

> "Just as prisoners tend not to believe in or desire the guards' rules and scrutiny but internalize them anyway, so many women may be disciplined by the "patriarchal gaze", irrespective of their own ideological frameworks. The number of feminists who find themselves removing "unwanted" body hair or dieting is, perhaps, an example of this process."[42]

Power is exercised here not from above but through a continual adjustment to norms and in continuing these practices individuals construct themselves as subjects. Naomi Wolf in *The Beauty Myth* (1991) describes what she perceives to be the new oppressive images of women in the 80s and 90s, as a patriarchal backlash to the earlier wave of white feminism of the 60s and 70s. The substitute for Betty Friedan's "happy housewife" of the 50s and 60s is the gaunt, youthful, white model and an oppressive image of the ideal female form. The bottom line of The Beauty Myth is "to buy more things for the body" and Wolf charts the growth of the $33 billion thinness industry, $20 billion cosmetic industry and $300 million cosmetic surgery industry. And the further effects: the enormous growth in North America and Europe in female anorexia and bulimia. She quotes Jane Fonda on her twenty-three history of bulimia: "[S]ociety says we have to be thin, and while most of us don't have much control over our lives, we can control our weight".[43] This cultural norm of appearance is enforced not only through the self-regulating subject but also through informal and formal

---

[41] See J. Berger, *Ways of Seeing* (1972) p. 47.
[42] See D. Cooper, *Power in Struggle: Feminism, Sexuality and the State* (1995) p. 14.
[43] Quoted in W. Chapkis, *Beauty Secrets* (1986), p. 11.

enforcement of appearance norms in the workplace.[44] Some feminists argue that images of women in advertising may be related to spousal abuse and violence against women.[45]

There is, therefore, the important role of everyday images and representations in contributing to harm and oppression. Stereotyped images in the private sphere of consumption may reinforce images of women in the public sphere of work and affect the way in which men respond in the private sphere of personal relationships. Critics of sex-role stereotyping argue that the demeaning images of women in the advertising media constrained the entry of women into public life and full participation in social life. The overlapping nature of these spheres calls into question the sharp distinction between private and public spheres, the non-political and the political. Individuals' preferences and tastes in both spheres are affected by the permissions and prohibitions on images in the media. An important goal of feminism has been, therefore, to subvert the "whole cultural landscape which, whether in selling carpet sweepers, collecting census information or uncovering women's crotches, place women as a subordinate sex".[46]

Feminist analysis underlines the importance of discourse in constituting womens subjectivity. The importance of discourse in creating influential images of women, from the "happy housewife" to the "superwoman", also underlines the fact that gender roles are contingent social constructions. There is not any essential conception of gender. In recent years advertising has made greater use of the male body as an erotic aspect of selling commodities and Mort argues that men are being encouraged to look at themselves as objects of consumer desire. He also speculates on whether this might lead to opportunities for subverting and transforming conceptions of masculinity. "As men (and as women) we carry a bewildering range of different and at times conflicting identities around with us in our heads at the same time".[47]

---

[44] See K. Klare, "Power/Dressing: Regulation of Employee Appearance" (1992) *New England Law Review* 1395 at 1421.

[45] See, *e.g.* J. Kilbourne, "Beauty ... and the beast of advertising" (1989) *Media and Values* 8.

[46] Lynne Segal, "Does Pornography cause violence?" in *Dirty Looks: Women Pornography Power* (P. Gibson and R. Gibson eds. 1993), p. 7.

[47] F. Mort, "The Politics of Consumption" in *New Times: The Changing Face of Politics in the 1990s* (S. Hall and M. Jacques eds., 1989) p. 169 and see F. Mort, *Culture of Consumption: Masculinities and Social Space in Late Twentieth-Century Britain* (1996).

Mort argues that there are opportunities for subverting dominant norms of masculinity, since identities are socially constructed. Consumption practices may be a site for resistance to existing social classifications. This approach stresses the active role of consumers in playing with meanings, using them for their own purposes and pleasures and resisting preferred meanings. This conception of the active consumer contrasts with the vision of the passive consumer, subject to the false consciousness of consumer capitalism. The idea of a true or false identity is rejected for a fluid and changing subjectivity. This approach is linked to the post-modern conception of the "decentred subject", constructing new forms of individuality out of the discourses of consumer capitalism.

The idea that we can actively choose identities, confounding dominant conceptions of class, gender and race, might be seen as related to the popular discourse of the citizen as consumer, in turn equated with choice and empowerment. Consumption practices may be what Foucault describes as a site of resistive power "the pleasure that kindles at having to evade ... power, flee from it, foil it or travesty it".[48] Oppositional discourse may be constructed from the bricolage of popular culture.

A recent argument has been that dress, appearance, the use of cosmetics, and "sexy dressing"[49], *i.e.* female dress practices which "deviate in the direction of sexiness from the norm" may be used to play with gender roles, subverting traditional ideas of gender and femininity. By showing the artificiality of gender, they may stir up what Judith Butler describes as "Gender trouble",[50] provoking resistance and bringing about emancipatory change. "Sexy dressing" may be used to challenge traditional patriarchal codes which state that women should only excite men sexually in situations where they are explicitly or implicitly inviting men to have access to them sexually.[51] It challenges both the assumption that "[s]he was asking for it", and also stereotypes which classify women as Madonna and whore, respectable and slut. A further aspect is to view practices such as cosmetic surgery as potentially

---

[48] M. Foucault, *The History of Sexuality* (1978) vol.1 trans. R. Hurley p. 45.
[49] See D. Kennedy "Sexual Abuse, Sexy Dressing and the Eroticization of Domination" in *Sexy Dressing* (D. Kennedy ed. 1993), Chap. 4.
[50] See J. Butler, *Gender Trouble* (1990).
[51] Kennedy, *op. cit.*, n. 49.

emancipatory. Cosmetic surgery is "first and foremost ... about taking one's life into one's own hands".[52]

These ideas have often focused on one of the most high profile exponents of this genre, Madonna, who according to Camille Paglia "is the future of feminism".[53]

> "Madonna is the true feminist. She exposes the puritanism and suffocating ideology of American feminism, which is stuck in an adolescent whining mode. Madonna has taught young women to be fully female and sexual while still exercising control over their lives. She shows girls how to be attractive, sensual, energetic, ambitious, aggressive, and funny—all at the same time".[54]

Madonna is celebrated here as providing a model of a woman in control of her own sexuality who "defied rather than rejected the male gaze" and shows ability to "explore ... various ways of constituting identities that refuse stability, that remain fluid, that resist definition".

Susan Bordo[55] is sceptical as to whether Madonna does escape from normalising discourse in which women are constructed as sexual objects. She points out how certain ideas about women and sexuality are embedded in our culture, for example, the woman as sexual temptress, enticing men through her body so that they cannot help but rape. Advertisements are situated within a continuing and powerful normalising discourse of the "continuing containment, sexualisation, and objectification of the female body" and the "continuing social realities of dominance and subordination".[56] She does not deny that people may get pleasure from alternative images or individual agency but that individuals should not mistake pleasure for political action challenging dominant normalising imagery. Her argument is that these oppressive images are deeply embedded culturally so that there is unlikely to be any "quick fix" through altering images in advertising as proposed by many liberal feminists who challenge sex-role stereotyping. Her argument echoes Gramsci's argument that common sense in a society often

---

[52] Bordo *op. cit.*, p. 20 quoting K. Davis, "Remaking the She-Devil: A Critical Look at Feminist Approaches to Beauty" (1991) 6:2 *Hypatia* 23.
[53] C. Paglia, *Sex Art and American Culture* (1992), p. 5.
[54] *ibid.*, p. 4.
[55] See S. Bordo *op. cit.*, n. 38 Part 3 "Material Girl: The Effacements of Postmodern Culture".
[56] *ibid.*, p. 275.

has deep roots in oppressive structures so that it is not a simple task to challenge the commonsense of cultural domination.

Bordo asks the following question:

"Just how helpful, for example, is an emphasis on creative agency in describing the relations of women and their bodies to the image industry of post-industrial capitalism, a context in which addictive bingeing and purging, exercise compulsions, and 'polysurgical addictions' are flourishing? Do we have a multi-million dollar industry in corrective surgery because people are asserting their racial and ethnic identities in resistance to prevailing norms, or because they are so vulnerable to the power of these norms? ... Admittedly, relentlessly focusing on cultural normalization can be depressing. It is exciting and hope inspiring to believe, rather that 'resistance is everywhere'."[57]

Bordo also argues that the decentring of the subject may not be liberating but extremely disorienting. The decentred individual may be even more vulnerable to whatever palliatives are served up by the culture industry. She is deeply critical of the extent to which commercial exploitation of cultural norms around women's bodies are portrayed as "self-determination and creative self-fashioning". For example, sports shoe manufacturers have recently stressed the potentially subversive nature of their products. Their advertisements to young women invite them to be in control of their body and to challenge the status quo. In fact, the representation of the body of the model in the advertisement is still of a perfect body with which the woman is invited to compare her own form.

Judith Williamson exhibits a similar distrust of fashion as resistance. She remarks pointedly that:

"Wearing a Lacoste sweatshirt doesn't make anyone middle class any more than wearing legwarmers makes you a feminist. The idea that ideologies— including consumer fads—are increasingly 'cut loose' from the economic base has become more and more fashionable on the academic left at a time when these levels have perhaps rarely been more obviously connected."[58]

The difficulties of developing oppositional cultural production are

---

[57] Bordo, *op. cit.*, p. 295.
[58] J. Williamson, "The Politics of Consumption" in *Consuming Passions: The Dynamics of Popular Culture* (J. Williamson ed., 1986) 229 at 233.

discussed in relation to representations of black female sexuality by bell
hooks. She discusses how the image of Tina Turner was developed by
her abusive partner within the tradition of the white cultural norm of
"the black female sexual savage", as expendable sexually available
object. Turner in her solo career has changed this image to that of the
"autonomous black woman whose sexuality is solely a way to exert
power ... she places herself in the role of the dominator".[59] But hooks
argues that Turner's model of the autonomous black female is still
rooted in misogyny since her sexuality is now about using her power
to do violence to males. Moreover hooks also argues that the equation
of sex with commodity exchange in her famous song "What's Love got
to do with it" evoked the equation of black sexuality with prostitution.
hooks underlines the difficulties facing black women's attempts to
assert an autonomous sexuality in the face of dominant racist cultural
stereotypes. Moreover she is critical of the attempts since the 1970s to
include positive images of black people in the culture industry. She
points out that previous to this period, the media and its portrayal of
blacks was often a site for critical discussion within her home of the
politics of race. She argues that since the 1970s the commodification
of black images by the media has hampered serious cultural critique.
"Placing cultural critiques by black critics solely in the reformist realm
of debate about good and bad images effectively silenced more complex
critical dialogue."[60]

The comments of Bordo and hooks underline the extent to which
images and representations in advertising and the media draw on
dominant and powerful cultural ideas which reinforce oppression and
domination and which may not be prone to any "quick fix". Thomson
argues that there is the danger that a preoccupation with diversity and
difference may "fail to take full account of the fact that, in the
actual circumstances of modern societies, diversity and difference are
commonly embedded in social relations which are structured in systematically asymmetrical ways".[61] These writers raise questions about
strategies to challenge cultural domination. They indicate that potentially alternative images may simply be co-opted and commodified to
serve the dominant culture. Feminist ideas of control over one's body

---

[59] b. hooks, "Selling hot Pussy" in *Black Looks: Race and Representation* (1992), p. 68.
[60] b. hooks "Liberation Scenes" in *Yearning* (1990), p. 5.
[61] J. Thomson, *Ideology and Modern Culture* (1990), pp. 330–331.

are translated into the need to buy running shoes so that one will be in perfect shape.

Haug in his *Critique of Commodity Aesthetics* argued that this ability to provide new grist for the commodity mill, was one of the functions of alternative culture:

> "some opposition groups among the young are highly productive for capital in an informal way. They consider their lifestyle to be set apart from the establishment; in so far as they make questions of appearance in lifestyle a point of criticism, they continually develop new appearances which are for a time their own—intended to identify them as a group—but which are constantly expropriated".[62]

4 Taste, Class and Cultural Critique: Bourdieu and Cultural Capital

A traditional distinction is to separate consumption which meets material needs and consumption which is undertaken for social reasons such as style, snobbery, and lifestyle. In fact, almost all consumption may be understood as connected to cultural or social values. Consumption is as much a symbolic as a material practice. This was one of the central points of Thorstein Veblen's *Theory of the Leisure Class* (1899). This book is sometimes viewed as a satirical critique of the "conspicuous consumption" among the new rich of the U.S. Eastern seaboard towards the end of the nineteenth century. From this perspective, the choices of this group provided an irrational exception to the generally rational process of consumption choices. In fact, Veblen's argument was that *all* consumption was embedded in social and cultural norms and practices and reflected social differentiation. "No class of society, not even the most abjectly poor, forgoes all customary conspicuous consumption".[63] All markets are cultural constructs and all consumption is shot through with cultural elements. The idea of the consumer as Robinson Crusoe, reflected in the development of neo-classical economics, neglected the interdependent nature of consumption decisions.

---

[62] W. Haug *Critique of Commodity Aesthetics* (1986), p. 90.
[63] T. Veblen, *The Theory of the Leisure Class* (1899), p. 70.

This argument was fundamental because it undercut the distinction between authentic needs and artificial needs, and the separation of the economic and cultural sphere. His argument was developed by later anthropologists who stressed the importance of consumption goods as symbolic necessities in all societies.[64]

This approach to consumption was systematically developed by Pierre Bourdieu, in his book *Distinction: A Social Critique of the Judgment of Taste* (1979, English translation, 1986). Bourdieu argues that taste, as reflected in an individual's preferences for an array of cultural goods and services, from food to music and sport, represent neither the arbitrary preferences of the economic model, nor the imposed values of the system of production. Consumption distinctions are part of social class differentiation, and taste for both high and popular culture is based on a complex amalgam of education, occupation, gender and class. Taste is a structural attribute, whose classificatory principles Bourdieu describes as a *habitus*, which are related to class divisions. Individuals assimilate this underlying *habitus* and then apply it throughout their varied consumption activities which will in turn reflect these classifications. They are rarely aware of these dispositions which allow them to identify individuals with similar taste. Culture also functions as a form of capital which legitimises social differentiation. The consumption of goods become not merely a reflection, but an instrument of class distinction.[65] These distinctions may be found in such apparently innocuous examples as parental preferences for childrens' toys. Daniel Miller summarises the argument: "[the] middle-class children's toy is never intended for mere amusement ... its prime interest is its educational value, the child must absorb the toy as a challenge, something from which it will learn in order to improve itself".[66]

Struggles over consumption and culture reflect class struggles between and within classes. Bourdieu argues that there is often a tension between the holders of economic capital, identified with business, and those holding cultural capital, that is, primarily educators and the chattering classes.[67] Attempts to alter cultural meanings which challenge existing

[64] See M. Douglas and B. Isherwood, *The World of Goods* (1979).
[65] D. Miller, *Material Culture and Mass Consumption* (1987), p. 153.
[66] *ibid.*, p. 153.
[67] Bourdieu comments that "All ... agents in a given social formation share a basic perceptual schemes, which receive the beginnings of objectification in the pairs of antagonistic objectives commonly used to classify and qualify persons or objects in the most varied area of practice. The network of oppositions between high (sublime,

cultural classifications, are likely to be politically contentious. Bourdieu's analysis is not reductionist in a purely economic sense and it recognises consumption as a relatively autonomous form of activity.[68] Tastes are not determined by class position but structures may limit them. Bocock provides the following example:

"There are major differences ... between the working classes' modes of consuming foods, drinks, television viewing, videos, home furnishings and decoration, cars and clothing, and those of the lower middle classes. Where the latter aim at respectability, and at picking up cues from 'higher' middle-class groups about how and what to consume, the working classes are more interested 'to have a good time', in direct pleasures. The income of some working-class households may well be higher than that of many lower middle-class households; but it is cultural, symbolic, factors which affect their consumption patterns, not income alone, according to Bourdieu".[69]

There are several important implications of Bourdieu's analysis. First, his approach contrasts with the image in some post-modern thought of the free-floating subject, choosing identities. The value of his work is the painstakingly detailed manner of his investigation which builds up a complex picture of how everyday trivia, such as eating habits, sports, aesthetic dispositions, habits in entertaining, promote structural social solidarity, differentiation and conflict. Cultural practices of everyday life are an important aspect of maintaining power and domination in society. This seems to suggest that one should be hesitant about reading too much into arguments that individuals can radically change their lives through changing habits in the marketplace, such as through fashion and lifestyle. While Bourdieu recognises the relative autonomy of consumption he sees greater cultural structure which is related to material power and material position in society. The decentred subject suggests freedom and choice whereas Bourdieu is denying the idea

---

elevated, pure) and low (vulgar, low, modest), spiritual and material, fine (refined, elegant) and coarse (heavy, fat, crude, brutal) ... between unique (rare, different, distinguished, exclusive, exceptional, singular, novel) and common (ordinary, banal, commonplace, trivail, routine), brilliant (intelligent) and dull (obscure, grey, mediocre), is the matrix of all the commonplaces which find such ready acceptance because behind them lies the whole social order ... The network has its ultimate source in the opposition between the elite and the dominated." P. Bourdieu, *Distinction: A Social Critique of the Judgment of Taste* (1986), p. 468.

[68] See R. Bocock, *Consumption* (1993), p. 64.

[69] *ibid.*, p. 64.

that in a consumer society there has developed much greater mobility of individuals across classes. He argues that the rise in mass education has not led to greater social mobility but that certain forms of cultural capital, usually dominant in middle–class backgrounds, when combined with education, continue to structure individuals' opportunities in life.

Bordieu's analysis that culture, both high and low, is intimately related to class distinctions forces us to think carefully through critiques of popular culture and associated practices such as advertising. For example, to what extent do criticisms of mass culture, (a recurring theme in the USA) simply reflect the taste of upper-middle class intellectuals or bourgeois fears of "the masses" rather than a serious political critique of the role of culture in sustaining cultural domination?[70] In a different context, conservative academics in North American universities defend "the canon" of great works of literature, and approved methods of reading these texts, against the introduction into the curriculum of books describing the experiences of immigrant workers. Should this be viewed as a fear of loss of cultural capital?

While there may be difficulties in transplanting Bourdieu's analysis of French society in the 1960s to North America, his work provides a valuable perspective on debates over culture and I discuss in Chapter 4 the applicability of his analysis to debates over television advertising to children. Bourdieu's analysis was a critique of the French middle classes but it could be used to support contemporary neo-liberal arguments that criticisms of advertising reflect the prejudices of middle and upper-middle class elites.

His arguments also suggest that it may very significant *who* is involved in making decisions about images and advertising, since assumptions about such issues will reflect social differentiation. There has been much written in England about the class position of judges in relation to issues of production and the rights of labour. But we might also want to scrutinise closely judicial approaches in the field of consumption practices. For example, in the case of *Harlingdon and Leinster Enterprise v. Christopher Hull Fine Art*[71] concerning a German expressionist painting which turned out to be a forgery, at least one judge is eager to impress the reader with his extensive knowledge of the world of fine art and the culture of the fine art market. But one wonders how he would react

---

[70] See Bourdieu, *op. cit.*, pp. 468–469.
[71] [1990] 1 A.E.R. 737.

to a discussion of the interpretation of the visual implications of Madonna's rendition of "Like a Virgin". The distinction between art and obscenity, between haute cuisine and low cuisine, abstract and popular art, are all related to cultural classificatory principles which embody social differentiation. Judicial approaches to commercial advertising may be embedded in a particular set of cultural classifications.

Summary: Implications of Cultural Studies

There are several points which may be summarised at this point.

First, cultural studies suggests a complex understanding of power in social life. In Chapter 2, I described existing narratives as viewing advertising as merely information or as being in a hierarchical relationship to the consumer. Cultural studies may lead us beyond conceptions of advertising as information or imposed power. It rejects the conception of consumers as puppets of propaganda but is also sceptical of a conception of them as "cheerful autonomous individuals just trying to have a good time".[72] Power circulates through media such as advertising, shaping our consciousness, but not through a simple imposition of ideas. We actively and routinely "buy in" to the messages of consumer capitalism but there also appears possibilities for resistance.

The analysis suggests that we may be "buying in" to several layers of messages. At one level is the persuasive message to purchase the product. Individuals may reject that message but still be affected by the symbolic message associating the commodity with a particular lifestyle. The advertisement may also invite us to reproduce secondary meanings in the advertisements concerning social relations in society, conceptions of ourselves and others. These images play a constitutive role in determining individual subjectivity.

There is often disagreement as to whether advertising is merely reflecting society or shaping society. Neither of these approaches captures the constitutive role of advertising in inviting individuals to reproduce the visions of social relations in advertising. They are the routine of consumer capitalism and we rarely stop to think about how

[72] See M. Berube, "Pop Goes the Academy: Cult Studs Fights the Power" *Voice Literary Supplement*.

we read them. They are both trivial and fundamental. The social relations dealt with by advertising on this routine basis are often important public issues such as race and gender relations, the portrayal of foreigners and images of our relationships with them. By inviting us to unthinkingly reproduce the values in the advertising it cannot be said to be merely a reflection of society. The ubiquity of advertising may create barriers to a serious understanding of important public issues, apart from its continuing ability to transfer ideas from the public realm such as democracy and equality to the private realm of the market. Historians argue that advertising has always tried to "muddle meanings".[73] Democracy and personal autonomy were associated with the ownership of commodities, particular visions of the family, ideas about individualism and the role of women. Advertising was one factor in affecting the construction of the cultural categories of public and private, family and market.

In the dominant approach to advertising regulation, the distinction between the public and the private sphere is central to thinking about the role of legal regulation of advertising. It is also part of popular discourse of the media so that one encounters statements such as "the government should not meddle in the private market" or "intrude into family life". Arguments against regulation of advertising often draw upon this imagery in terms of arguments about intervention in the private market, or intervention in the realm of private decision-making by parents (*e.g.* see below the discussion of childrens' advertisements) or consumers. But cultural analysis suggests that this structure of thought is inadequate for analysing regulation of advertising. Advertising plays a central role in the inextricable linking of economy and culture, and the public and the private sphere in consumer capitalism. Family life, sexuality, personal presentation and appearance are all important topics of advertising discourse stressing the connections between the appropriateness of particular norms of self-regulation and good citizenship.

Secondly, the conception of the socially situated subject who both produces and is a product of social norms and linguistic codes suggests a different way of thinking about issues concerning advertising than is currently provided by the dichotomy of free choice versus paternalism

---

[73] T. Jackson Lears, "Some Versions of Fantasy: Toward a Cultural History of American Advertising, 1880–1930" *Prospects IX* 349 at 352.

and rationality versus manipulation. The recognition of the extent to which social life is continually constituted and reproduced through individual behaviour underlines the difficulties of separating structure and agency in modern life.

Thirdly, Bourdieu's analysis highlights the fact that, contrary to the maxim *de gustibus non est disputandum*, taste and culture are indeed important political issues and consumption is a significant site of political action. But he also makes one aware of the danger of confusing serious cultural critiques of consumer capitalism with moralisms and moral panics. The fact that advertising may be tasteless or offensive to middle-class morality is not, without more, a particularly convincing basis for regulation. One of the effects of the mixing of economy and culture in modern society has been the gradual effacement of the high/low culture distinction. This undermines the possibility of authoritative cultural criticism of popular culture. The collapse of the high/low culture distinction does not mean that we are in a state of free-floating relativism. It does mean that it is always necessary to ask "how all representations are constructed, for what purpose, by whom, and with what components".[74]

Bourdieu's insights on cultural capital emphasise that battles over culture reflect intra- and inter-class conflict. Concerns among the intellectual classes about "levelling down" and middle-class critiques of the "wasteland" of television may be partly intra-class disputes between different forms of capital, economic (business) and cultural (as represented by professionals, university academics and so on), each attempting "to project its interests, its "capital", as the proper source for social reputation and status."[75] Historical scholarship has shown the use of consumption practices as forms of social control, as exercised through sumptuary laws or the French courtly traditions.[76]

If we should be wary of endorsing every critique of popular culture, nonetheless, the development of a concentrated "culture industry", combining economy and culture, does raise many questions. While anti-trust law addresses the issue of economic monopoly and exclusion, there has been no similar legal regulation of cultural monopolies, dominant positions or exclusions. Indeed, the law of trademarks and unfair competition fiercely protects the cultural symbols of multinational

---

[74] E. Said. *Culture and Imperialism* (1993), p. 314.
[75] R. Bocock and K. Thompson eds. *Social and Cultural Forms of Modernity* (1992) p. 164.
[76] See the discussion of these issues in Rosalind Williams, *Dream Worlds* (1982).

capital. Whatever oppositional discourse may develop within the interstices of these symbols, it is these industries which have successfully
established the ground rules of the system.

Fourthly, cultural theories are interpretive rather than scientific in
the positivistic sense. The law is also an interpretive endeavour, which
provides authoritative stories about the social world. In the area of
advertising regulation the court is often required to interpret the
meaning of an advertisement and to assess the effects of advertising.
Does it mislead this particular group? Does it affect consumption
decisions? Empirical evidence is often remarkably limited and ambiguous on such issues and cultural studies suggests that texts and images
may not have fixed meanings. But we do not expect courts to be merely
readers of social science evidence. They are important interpreters of
public and political values and their decisions reflect cultural battles
over public norms. Cultural studies indicates that there are a number
of structures for reading advertisements. Perhaps judges and regulators
might draw on this form of knowledge in developing law's truth about
advertising.

Finally, much of advertising concerns symbols and images. Consumers make connections between images and products. In many
contemporary advertisements there may be little written text. They
may not even mention the product and the text of the advertisement
will take its meaning(s) from interaction with the images. The issue of
regulation is, therefore, posed in terms of the regulation of images but
most analysis continues to focus on the regulation of words and
interpretation of texts. Catherine Mackinnon titles her most recent text
on pornography "Only Words" but it is primarily concerned with the
harm created by pornographic images. Regulation of images is fraught
with difficulty but again the law might turn to cultural analyses of
images in developing its truth.

Chapter 4

A Cultural Perspective on Legal Doctrine

This chapter analyses several areas of advertising law. These are: the distinction between the reasonable and the credulous consumer standards in the law of misleading advertising; the doctrine of commercial speech which extends constitutional protection of freedom of expression to advertising messages; the regulation of advertising to children and the regulation of harmful advertising images of women and minorities. These topics are not only of current practical interest in many countries, but also raise politically contested questions about the role of advertising regulation, illustrate competing cultural visions of consumer markets and expose the material interests and values at stake in contests over the role of consumerism in contemporary life. They illustrate also the important constitutive role of advertising law in constructing the legal subject of consumer law and the relation of this subject to ideologies which sustain cultural domination in terms of class, gender and race. My purpose is both critique and construction. I employ a cultural perspective to probe existing understandings of the issues at stake in each area, the blind spots of current analyses, and the implications of insights from cultural studies for understanding the relevant doctrine. A general theme is whether it is possible or desirable to develop a theory of advertising law based on concepts of cultural power and domination. This requires some reflection on the cultural role of law and the record of the law in policing cultural images.

1 The Reasonable and the Credulous: Gender, Credulity and "The Other" in Advertising Law

A central doctrinal question in misleading advertising law concerns the standard of deception. The issue is whether an advertisement will give rise to liability even if it would not deceive reasonable consumers, but would deceive a credulous or trusting person. Liability under the credulous person test is sometimes disparagingly referred to as the "fools test" based on the comment in a famous U.S. case that advertising should be clear enough so that "in the words of the prophet Isaiah, 'wayfaring men, though fools shall not err therein' ".[1] In recent years there has been much criticism of the idea that the law should protect naive or gullible consumers. It is argued that protection of this supposedly small group may deprive the majority of consumers of valuable information and represents unjustified paternalism. Although the choice of the relevant standard might seem a relatively modest question of public policy, it is a politically contested issue in advertising law in both North America and Europe. The European Court of Justice disagrees with the German Federal Supreme Court,[2] and the Federal Trade Commission split over the desirability of protecting only reasonable consumers. There was a heated debate at the Commission in the early 1980s over proposals that would only sanction misleading representations which are "likely to mislead consumers acting reasonably under the circumstances".[3] After adoption of this formula by a majority of commissioners, a dissenting Commissioner argued that the adoption of such a standard would permit exploitation by a small segment of business which "makes its livelihood preying upon consumers who are very trusting and unsophisticated".[4]

---

[1] *Charles of the Ritz Distributors Corp. v. FTC* 143 F.2d. 676, at 680 (2d. Cir. 1944) citing to *General Motors Corp. v. FTC* 114 F.2d. 33 (2nd. Circ. 1940), at 36.

[2] See, *e.g.* Case C-315/92, *Verband Sozialer Wettbewerb v. Clinique Lab. & Estee Lauder Cosmetics:* [1994] I E.C.R. 317. The use of "Clinique" trademark would not confuse or mislead reasonable consumers as to the health properties of the cosmetic. The product had been marketed as Clinique in all countries of the EU except Germany where it was marketed as "Linique". See N. Reich, "The 'November Revolution' of the European Court of Justice: Keck, Meng and Audi Revisited" (1994) C.M.L.R. 459 at 483–485.

[3] The policy statement is reprinted in an appendix to *Re Cliffdale Associates Inc.* 103 F.T.C. 110 at 174 (1984). See also P. Bailey and M. Pertschuk, "The Law of Deception: The Past as Prologue" (1984) 33 *American University L. Rev.* 849.

[4] Commissioner Pertschuk in *Re Cliffdale Associates Inc.* 103 FTC 110 (1984) at 186 (1984).

A common theme in feminist and cultural studies is the critique of the concept of the liberal legal subject. Bartlett and Kennedy comment that:

"The Anglo-US system presupposes what is essentially a mythical being: a legal subject who is coherent, rational, and freely choosing, and who can, in ordinary circumstances, be held fully accountable for his actions. Thus, legal doctrines generally assume that an individual acts with clear intentions that are transparently available to himself and to others, on the basis of suppositions about what a 'rational person' would do in similar circumstances."[5]

The law of misleading advertising starts from the norm of liberal individualism outlined above while conceding that certain consumers may not match up to the standard. When the law does protect the credulous it is often conceptualised as a protection for the weak or the vulnerable, thus suggesting that individuals, either momentarily because of high pressure selling, or because of their limited capacities, are acting irrationally and need the paternalistic protection of the law. Those constructed as credulous consumers have often been women or working-class consumers.[6] These facts of class and gender are often omitted in commentaries and texts in consumer law. There is here perhaps an intersection between doctrinal assumptions concerning the protection of a "weak unfortunate person, however gullible",[7] and cultural associations of consumption with supposedly feminine characteristics of passivity and impulsiveness, contrasting with the rationality of the supposedly male virtues associated with production. Consumer markets are potentially dangerous sites for subversion of these values of rationality and for loss of control. Selling is often equated with seduction[8]

---

[5] K. Bartlett and R. Kennedy, ed. *Feminist Legal Theory: Readings in Law and Gender* (1991), p. 7.

[6] A short list of examples include, *e.g.* Louisa Carlill in *Carlill v. Carbolic Smoke Ball Co.*, Pearl Elizabeth Goldthorpe in *Goldthrope v. Logan*. Gladys Escola in *Escola v. Coca Cola Bottling Co.* 150 P.2d. 436 (1944). The central cases on the credulous person test in the USA deal with womens' products. See below, *Charles of the Ritz v. FTC*, *Gelb v. FTC and Aronberg v. FTC*. See further I. Ramsay, "Consumer Law and Structures of Thought: A Comment" (1993) 16 *Journal of Consumer Policy* 79 at 90 (working-class consumers described as "decent, simple people").

[7] *Goldthorpe v. Logan* [1943] 2 D.L.R. 519, C.A. The court held a company liable where they had promised in advertisements that their facial hair removal treatment was "guaranteed". Protection for the female consumer was grounded in a collateral warranty.

[8] "[S]elling is still equated with seduction, advertisers with seducers, women with their prey" Jackson Lears, *Fables of Abundance: A Cultural History of Advertising in America* (1994), p. 72.

and the law continues to refer to "the techniques of seduction in advertising".[9] The common law doctrine of *caveat emptor* as announced by Holmes J. in relation to puffing (see above Chapter 2) could be seen as the need to hold fast to "manly virtues" in markets, resisting the embellishments of the seductive puff. Feminist writers have drawn similarities between the social construction of legal values in law and masculinity. Both seem to celebrate "rationality, reason, ... objectivity and abstract and principled activity".[10] Ideas of rational choice embedded in the law may be contrasted with the credulity and gullibility of "the other", the consumer who may need the paternalistic protection of the father figure of the law, a patriarchal rather than empathetic paternalism.

One of the most famous "credulous consumers", at least in the eyes of contemporary commentators on the case, was Louisa Carlill, the middle-class female plaintiff in the famous English case of *Carlill v. The Carbolic Smoke Ball Co.*[11] Louisa Carlill contracted influenza notwithstanding her use of the smoke ball which had been advertised as a prophylactic for influenza. The English court of appeal held the company contractually liable to Carlill for the £100 reward which they had advertised would be paid to any person contracting influenza after inhaling the smoke ball as directed in their instructions. In his fascinating account of the background to the case Brian Simpson indicates that Carlill was encouraged to sue by her spouse, who had at one time practiced as a solicitor and who was "exasperated" by the level of absurdity of the advertisements of the period.[12] The Carbolic Smoke Ball had been advertised in North America[13] and the United Kingdom.

Newspaper commentary at the time clearly thought that the courts had protected a gullible consumer. The Pall Mall Gazette (original publishers of the advertisement) commented that "for once advertisers have counted too much on the gullibility of the public", and a leader in *The Lancet* noted that:

---

[9] See, *e.g.* Dickson C.J. in *Irwin Toy v. Attorney General of Quebec op. cit.*, Chap. 1, n. 20.
[10] Thornton, "Feminist jurisprudence: illusion or reality?" 3 *Australian Journal of Law and Society* 5 at 7, cited in Smart, *op. cit.*, p. 86.
[11] [1893] 1 Q.B. 256, C.A.
[12] A.W.B. Simpson, "Quackery and Contract Law: The Case of the Carbolic Smoke Ball" (1985) 14 *Journal of Legal Studies* 345.
[13] Simpson indicates that it is not known whether the Smoke Ball was marketed in America. One of my colleagues provided me with an advertisement for the Smoke Ball from the Toronto *Globe and Mail*.

"People who are silly enough to adopt a medicine simply because a tradesman is reckless enough to make extravagant promises and wild representations as to its efficiency may thank themselves chiefly for any disappointment that ensues. Still for this folly, which is only foolish and nothing worse, it is possible to feel sympathy when the disappointment comes. It is a pleasant alternative to learn that the dupe has been able, in the present instance, to enforce a sharp penalty."

The *Spectator* argued that no man would have pressed the claim and that Mrs Carlill had showed "all that patient determination and persistent importunity of which only a woman is capable".[14]

The doctrinal explanation of her success in overcoming the puffing doctrine is attributed by many legal texts to the deposit of £1000 in the Alliance Bank, Regent Street to show the sincerity of the advertisers. This indicated that the promise was intended seriously and was not a "mere puff". But it is questionable whether the deposit of the money added much to the seriousness of the claim. It might be interpreted by the smart reader as simply underlining the bizarre and exaggerated nature of the promises which were extremely common in advertisements for patent medicines at this time. It may well have strained the bounds of common sense to assume that it should be taken seriously, and this was clearly the opinion of the media.

Moreover, the consumerist values of "protection for the weak", emphasised in the lower court by Hawkins J.[15] were anomalous when compared with the approach of the courts to regulation of other markets. Lindley L.J., who delivered the strong leading judgment in *Carlill*, seemed to have little sympathy in other cases for investors who were gulled by relying on blatantly misleading prospectuses.[16] Only 20 years earlier, in *Derry v. Peek*, in addressing a situation bordering on securities fraud, the House of Lords had eviscerated the equitable conception of fraud. Atiyah commented that this case was "the final triumph of market principles in the law of contract. By confining the definition of fraud within the narrowest grounds possible, the law lords here insisted upon the obligations of those who bought and sold in the market, to rely upon their own judgment, and not upon opinions

---

[14] Quoted in Simpson *op cit.*, at 365.

[15] "Such advertisements do not appeal so much to the wise and thoughtful as to the credulous and weak portions of the community". [1892] 2 Q.B. 484, Hawkins J. at 488.

[16] See his comments in *Mckeown v. Boudard-Peveril Gear Co.* (1896) 65 L.J. 735 at 736.

proffered by the other party."[17] But Lindley L.J. in *Carlill* had no hesitation in rejecting out of hand the argument that the Smoke Ball advertisement was a puff or that no one would take the promise seriously. Bowen L.J. also had little time for such arguments: "... [i]f a person chooses to make extravagant promises of this kind he probably does so because it pays him to make them, and, if he has made them, the extravagance of the promises is no reason in law why he should not be bound by them".[18] As Trebilcock comments "[f]or 1893 and the supposed heyday of laissez faire and caveat emptor these are strong views indeed".[19] *Carlill* was one of the first cases to analyse the puffing doctrine in relation to mass marketing of consumer products. Previous cases had concerned statements by auctioneers concerning the sale of land, where individuals often had an opportunity to inspect the property,[20] and it had been applied also in the late nineteenth century to speculative stock market investments.

Carlill is often constructed by commentators as a bizarre or comical case, which accounts partly for its continuing survival in English texts and casebooks.[21] The emphasis is often on the curious nature of the product, and the credulity of the victim rather than the clearly fraudulent selling practices of a potentially dangerous product. Coupled with the absence of later litigation it may be viewed as an historical artefact which exposed the marketing practices on the periphery of the emerging modern marketplace. The judges may have been moved by class hostility to this fringe commercial operator, a tradition in consumer protection jurisprudence in the United Kingdom,[22] by their knowledge of the quackery in this industry, by the health aspects or the fact that

---

[17] P.S. Atiyah, *Rise and Fall of Freedom of Contract* (1979) at 673 where Atiyah notes that *Derry v. Peek* was decided by a House of Lords which did not include a single Chancery Law Lord and that "according to Pollock all of Lincoln's Inn thought the decision wrong".

[18] *Carlill op. cit.* at 268.

[19] M. Trebilcock, "Private law remedies for misleading advertising" (1972) 22 Univ. Toronto L.J. 1 at 4.

[20] See *Dimmock v. Hallett* (1866) L.R. 2 Ch. App. 21: *Scott v. Hanson* (1829) Russ and M.127. It is worthwhile to note that in both these cases the purchaser did in fact receive a remedy, although not based on the particular statement.

[21] Simpson, *op. cit.*, pp. 364, 375.

[22] See, *e.g.* the attitude of English judges to used car dealers under the Trade Descriptions Act 1968 in cases such as *R. v. Hammertons Cars* [1976] 1 W.L.R. 1243 (judgment of Lawton J.).

this was not a commercial gamble on the stock market. Perhaps it represented a protective but gendered paternalism.

Carlill was not, however, the only case dealing with fraudulent selling schemes of patent medicines. In a slightly later Scottish case Bile Bean Manufacturing Co. v. Davidson[23] the Court of Session refused to grant an injunction to the "Bile Bean Manufacturing Co" for trade mark infringement against a chemist, on the ground that the reputation of the bile beans had been established by what the Lord Justice Clerk described as "a gigantic and too successful fraud". The beans, known as "Bile Beans for Biliousness" were widely advertised using a common technique of the period ... "imperial primitivism".[24] This theme was that of the Caucasian entering a "primitive" land, finding a time-honoured natural remedy and bringing it back to civilisation. In this case the claim was that the pills contained natural vegetable substances from aboriginal Australians. All of this was completely false and in truth the "complainers had formed a scheme to palm off upon the public a medicine obtained from drug manufacturers in the US." They had flooded the English market with advertisements for the beans, spending £300,000 in advertising and selling expenses. The court rejected the argument that the statements concerning the pills were mere puffing but "were statements of alleged facts ... carefully elaborated ... from which the public might draw a sound inference that the article sold would affect to the buyers what it had done for ages to another race in another part of the world". It is interesting that in an action between two corporations there was no discussion of whether these claims would only be believed by the credulous. The focus was on the fraudulent selling practices.

The types of claim made in Carlill and Bile Beans dominated advertising of patent medicines at this time and often tapped into themes which seem remarkably modern. Jackson Lears describes how the possibility of rejuvenation, self-transformation and sexual regeneration were common themes in patent medicines advertisements.[25] Various devices could cure sexual lassitude or "weakness" in men. The Victorian fascination with sexuality was reflected in such remedies as "Kawa", a Peruvian remedy which cured "nervous and sexual debility" with an advertising line which stated: "[i]f you are about to marry, do not think

---

[23] (1906) 8 F.1181 (Court of Sesson).
[24] Lears, op. cit., p. 146.
[25] Lears, op. cit., Chap. 5.

lightly of the future. As you expect to have a woman for a wife, be sure that she has a man for a husband". Mosko's silver pills promised that "[e]lectricity is in every pill" and that on coming into contact with gastric juices made the individual "feel young again, to realise the joyous sparkle of nerve life as it infuses the body with its growing vitality; to feel the magnetic enthusiasm of youthful ambition".[26]

The excesses of patent medicine claims at the end of the nineteenth century led to the truth in advertising movement of the progressive era of the early twentieth century and the enactment of Food and Drug legislation in several countries. This was intended to introduce a greater rationality to the marketplace. But the themes of rejuvenation and the importance of personal attention to the most intimate details of one's body and personal appearance were continuing themes in advertising. The Foucauldian concept of "the self-regulating subject" was reflected in advertisements which increasingly insinuated normalising images of personal and physical perfection. Images of rejuvenation which had been used to sell patent medicines were attached to other products such as breakfast cereals.

It is questionable whether the promises of the patent medicines era differ significantly from the more modern promises associated with slimming and health claims. Surveying quack medicines in the 1950s Webster noted that "half a billion goes into the nutrition racket ... another quarter billion is spent for medicines and gadgets falsely purporting to promote recovery from arthritis and rheumatism. A hundred million goes for ineffective reducing remedies ..."[27] An example from the 1970s is a Canadian prosecution for misleading advertising which was brought against a firm trading as "Contour slim" for advertising a treatment which claimed to remove unwanted fat in 90 minutes. The advertising stated that all the consumer had to do was to "sit back in a comfortable sofa and relax while the Contour slim method does the work for you".[28] The treatment involved a body wrap soaked in a solution called "Bain de Mer Gaspé aux Algues Marine". (A bath in seaweed from the Gaspé region of Quebec). The treatment had no effect on weight loss. While convicting the company the judge indicated that "[t]he weak portion of the public, of which I am one, has to be protected in these matters". In 1995 the Federal Trade

---

[26] *Loc. cit.*, p. 144.
[27] J.H. Young, *The Toadstool Millionaires* (1961), p. 251.
[28] See *R. v. Contour Slim* (1972) 9 Canadian Criminal Cases 2d. 482.

Commission entered into a consent decree with "Nature's Bounty Inc" which had marketed diets which promoted weight loss during sleep, and a compound known as "New Zealand Green Lipped Mussel Extract" which claimed to prevent arthritis.[29] In 1995 the Advertising Standards Authority in the United Kingdom found 23 per cent of claims in a survey of health advertisements to be either dubious or breaches of the code. They noted that: "[m]any troublesome advertisements for therapies, offering all manner of things from orthopaedic furniture to impotency tablets stated that the product would cure the condition not simply relieve the symptoms".[30]

One might argue that these types of claims are on the periphery of the market and may involve fairly marginal enterprises. It is, however, not clear how distant these therapeutic claims are from the contemporary stock-in-trade claims of the cosmetic industry which advertise the rejuvenating nature of their products which contain such ingredients as "Extract of skin Caviar" or "re-nutriv souffle".[31] The central theme of rejuvenation in cosmetic advertising was the issue in a celebrated U.S. case of the 1940s, *Charles of the Ritz v. FTC.*[32] which is often cited as an illustration of the credulous person test, continues to be discussed in the major casebooks in consumer law in the United States and concerns an industry whose selling practices have changed little since the time of the decision.

From 1934 to 1939 Charles of the Ritz had marketed a cream known as "rejuvenescence", representing that it gave the skin a "wonderfully rejuvenating bloom". Over $1,000,000 in sales of the cream were made during this period. The Federal Trade Commission charged the company with making false representations, since no cosmetic could overcome the skin's ageing process. The Federal Circuit Court of Appeal rejected the company's defence that "no straight thinking person" would believe that its cream could actually rejuvenate. In the ringing words of Clark J:

"[the] law was 'not made for the protection of experts, but for the public— that vast multitude which includes the ignorant, the unthinking and the credulous' ... While the wise and worldly may well realize the fantasy of

---

[29] F.T.C. file no. 932 3224, press release, April 27, 1995.
[30] *ASA Monthly Report* No. 48.
[31] L. Savan, *The Sponsored Life* (1994) p. 208.
[32] 143 F. 2d. 676 (2d. Circuit, 1944).

any representations that the present product can roll back the years, there remains 'that vast multitude' of others who like Ponce de Leon, still seek a perpetual fountain of youth ... the average woman conditioned by talk in the magazines and over the radio of 'vitamins, hormones, and God knows what' might take 'rejuvenescence' to mean that this is one of the modern miracles and is something which would actually cause her youth to be restored."

How should we read this decision? One approach might be to view it as reflecting judicial deference to a public agency's mission to protect the weak, and the unwillingness of the court to second guess the agency's judgment on the need for protection. It might in hindsight be viewed as a heavily gendered paternalism. Women consumers are protected because they are unable to protect themselves. There is almost an analogy to the idea of incapacity as reflected in our treatment of children. This perspective is highly patronising and this case, which has come to stand for the credulous person test in advertising law, has been much criticised by commentators. Comments such as "does the holding in *Charles of the Ritz* ... indict the intelligence of the general public?"[33] and "would any reasonable person believe that rejuvenescence would make their skin young?"[34] may be found in leading U.S. consumer law texts.

Even stronger criticism is reserved for another decision of that period *Gelb et. al. v. Federal Trade Commission*,[35] described by one commentator as a "frequently cited, frequently ridiculed" decision.[36] In this case the Commission held that claims by the manufacturers of "Clairol" shampoo that, among other things, it coloured the hair permanently, were misleading since it had no effect upon new hair. The majority of the court was somewhat sceptical that any user would believe that this was the meaning of the term permanently but deferred to the Commission's findings since the Act was for the protection of the trusting as well as the suspicious. Clark J. commented that "the Commission has the bounden duty to take comparatively stern measures against this type of particularly crude, if not cruel, appeal to the human vanities".[37]

---

[33] J. Spanogle and R. Rohner, *Consumer Law* (1979) p. 61.
[34] M. Greenfield, *Consumer Transactions* (1983), p. 46.
[35] 144 F.2d. 580 (1944).
[36] R. Schechter, "The Death of the Gullible Consumer" (1989) University of Illinois L. Rev. 571 at 575.
[37] *ibid.*, p. 583.

The final case of note is *Aronberg v. FTC*[38] which concerned advertisements for pills for the relief of delayed menstruation, known as "Perio pills" and "Perio Relief compound". The Commission had claimed that the seller had claimed that the pills were effective, harmless remedies for such delay when in fact they were harmful and merely dealt with the symptoms of delayed menstruation but did not provide a remedy. The seller denied that any consumer would understand the advertisements as providing a remedy rather than merely relief of symptoms. The advertising claims included claims that:

"Delay Never Worries Me"

"Don't be alarmed over delayed, overdue, unnaturally suppressed periods. A new discovery—Triple X relief Compound is fastest acting, safest aid to married women. Acts without discomfort or inconvenience even in obstinate cases"

"Many Women Testify to its Relief for Delay. Why Dont you Do what so many other Women Do?"

"Thousands of women are needlessly miserable and unhappy because of abnormally delayed periods. If you are one of these troubled, discouraged women, lose no time in trying Perio Relief compound. Scores of women ... highly praise Perio Relief compound for its reputed effectiveness and the blessed relief it gives them ..."

"Much of the constant charm and loveliness of womanhood depends upon a regular occurrence of her periodic function. When a lapse of this vital function occurs ... her comfort is often disturbed by pain ... her disposition is apt to turn irritable. What is more, the happiness of those dear to her may be effected ... Perhaps you have been faced with this situation.
For countless women such unnatural interruption is often needless. To them a simple preparation is offered, which in many cases of abnormally suppressed, overdue, scant and painful periods has helped start the function, thus bringing gratifying relief. It is called Perio Relief compound and may be taken at home without, in most instance, interfering with daily activities".

The pills had potentially serious side-effects which were not indicated on the product packaging. The court agreed that to an educated analytical reader the claims would not be read as claiming anything more than the provision of relief:

---

[38] 132 F.2d. 165 (7th Cir. 1942).

"But the buying public does not ordinarily carefully study or weigh each word in an advertisement. The ultimate impression upon the mind of the reader arises from the sum total of not only what is said but also of what is reasonably implied ... the public ... are not, as a whole, experts in grammatical construction ... the law is not made for experts but to protect the public—that vast multitude which includes the ignorant, the unthinking and the credulous."[39]

The critiques of these decisions imply that the decisions were as foolish as the consumers being protected. It is assumed that no "rational" individual would be influenced by these claims or believe that they could provide a cure rather than merely relieve symptoms. These critiques never mention the fact that the products were used by women—the consumers are an abstract non-sexed group—nor do they mention the background or cultural context to the advertisements.

In his history of U.S. advertisements of this period, Marchand describes how the necessity of cultivating "a modern youthful look", primarily through the use of cosmetics, permeated advertising images of women. Advertising reminded women continually to look at themselves as objects being surveyed through men's gazes, stressed the "Beauty Contest of Life" and the importance of catching and holding "the springtime of her beauty":

"The warnings could be positively intimidating. 'What Do Men think when they look at you?' asked one Camay soap ad. 'You against the rest of Womankind; your beauty ... your charm ... your skin' warned another. 'Someone's eyes are forever searching your face, comparing you with other women'. "[40]

This result would be achieved, according to the advertisements through the triumph of modern science over the ageing process. In an analysis of Canadian advertising of this period, Mawhood notes that, "the preservation of youth through science—the assertion of human skills over the natural ageing process—was of paramount importance in advertising of the 1920s and 1930s. The irreversibility of the ageing process was a godsend for manufacturers of products of temporary

---

[39] ibid., p. 167.
[40] R. Marchand, *Advertising the American Dream: Making Way for Modernity 1920–1940* (1985), p. 176.

effect, such as hair dyes and depilatories".[41] Cosmetics and beauty were also sold as a method of achieving class mobility.

It was during the 1920s and thirties that the cosmetics industry grew significantly and helped to institutionalise a beauty culture which emphasised gender difference and was part of a reaction against the feminism of the earlier part of the century and the New Woman image of the 1920s. While some have seen the use of cosmetics as part of a potential liberatory model of women defined in terms of their capacity to consume,[42] there is also evidence that it was associated with oppressive normalising images, based on Anglo-Saxon models of feminine beauty.

An assumption in critiques of these decisions is that the credulous standard of deception may have been appropriate in the 1930s for an unsophisticated consumer audience, but that it has little place in the 1990s where consumers are better educated and sceptical of advertising claims. Yet contemporary writers such as Naomi Wolf in the *Beauty Myth* describe, in passages redolent of *Charles of the Ritz*, the modern "holy oils" which promise rejuvenation, commenting that "skin creams do not actually do anything. The holy oil industry is a megalith that for forty years has been selling women nothing at all". And she quotes an industry executive whose colleagues tell him:

"Women are so dumb. How can they buy all that grease and stuff? Educated women, who've been to Radcliffe and Cambridge and Oxford and the Sorbonne—what gets into them? Why do they go to Bloomingdales and pay $250 for that hokum?"[43]

The U.S. Food and Drug Administration took action in 1988 against cosmetic companies which claimed that their products were "anti-ageing", threatening to classify them as drugs since they made physiological claims. The response of the cosmetic companies was to change their advertising practices to state that creams reduced "the visible signs" of ageing. Whether this has had any more impact on the cosmetic industry than the decision in *Charles of the Ritz* is difficult to gauge.

These cases raise several general questions about advertising law and

---

[41] R. Mawhood, "Images of Feminine Beauty in Advertisements for Beauty Products, English Canada 1901–41." (Masters Thesis McGill University 1991) p. 88.
[42] See K. Piess, "Making Faces: the cosmetics industry and the cultural construction of gender, 1890–1930" (1990) 7 *Genders* p. 143.
[43] N. Wolf, *The Beauty Myth* (1991), pp. 109, 111.

the distinction between the rational and credulous. They pose the question of what the law assumes to be a rational purchase decision and whether the contrast between the rational and the credulous seems appropriate as a method of describing the issues at stake in the cases. We have already encountered the difficulty of deciding what is a rational consumer decision in the debate over artificial product differentiation. Critics of highly advertised brands argued that the symbolic associations with brands through image advertising led to economically irrational elements in consumer choices and that the "presence of irrational consumer allegiances may constitute a barrier to entry."[44] The response of neo-classical economists was that it was a rational choice, because of the information provided by the brand image.

It is not clear what a rational decision would be in relation to a cosmetic purchase. In *Charles of the Ritz* Clark J. assumes that rational purchasers would discount the claims of rejuvenescence but that the credulous consumer would fail to do so. But why would rational purchasers buy the product? It is surely not based upon a simple assessment of the ingredients of the cosmetics and its utilitarian characteristics. Stigler and Becker would reply that it was purchased to maximise utility which could include the distinction value of a youthful look. The utility must be measured by what the consumer does with the product: it is not an inherent characteristic of the product. Cultural theory would stress in slightly differing terms the idealistic aspect of consumption that "it is not the actual selection, purchase or use of products, but the imaginative pleasure seeking to which the product image lends itself, 'real consumption' being largely a resultant of this 'mentalistic' hedonism."[45]

When viewed from this perspective the issue in *Charles of the Ritz* is not one of deception, traditionally understood, unless one subscribes to a view of consumption as false consciousness. It could be phrased as a concern about "buying into" images connected to particular visions of appropriate female behaviour. From this perspective it is the potentially oppressive norms of gender and racial appearance associated with cosmetic advertising which are at issue. Bordo argues that these are not innocent images and can be connected to the growth of anorexia, bulimia and other eating disorders. Nor are they purely private since

---

[44] *Smith v. Chanel Inc.* 402 F.2d. 562 (1968) Browning J. at 121.
[45] C. Campbell, *The Romantic Ethic and the Spirit of Modern Consumerism* (1987), p. 187 quoted in K. Thompson, *Key Quotations in Sociology* (1996), p. 27.

they are connected to appearance regulation at work and in other public institutions. Post-modernism might view appearance as a site for subversion of these gendered norms but it would be naïve to underestimate the normalising power of these images. What is clear is that *Charles of the Ritz* is as much about unfair cultural practices as deceptive trade practices.

It is not clear, however, that law is an effective or appropriate tool for addressing such issues. Neither the paradigm of truth nor advertising as information seem to be tools suited to the task of regulation of these image claims. The individualistic premises of the law with its disembodied rational consumer, free of the inequalities of race, gender and social class, may be incapable of addressing cultural questions of oppression. The concept of manipulation is potentially demeaning. One solution would be to turn to interpretive analysis of the type discussed in Chapter 3. This indicates how advertisements invite consumers to buy into normalising images, and the manner in which consumers may actively reproduce damaging social images. Their analyses indicate that it is possible to develop a general cultural critique through the interpretation of individual images. There would undoubtedly be differing interpretations, but that is always a possibility with expert evidence. This approach would challenge law's dichotomy of rational/manipulation and the sharp distinction between the rational and credulous. Since all advertising images can be said to contribute to the constitution of an individual's subjectivity, the law would be faced with difficult questions of distinguishing between good and bad shaping. This would not necessarily be an easy question to answer but the tools exist to make an attempt. The fact that the law and lawyers have shown little interest in this form of analysis may be because of the continuing preference in law and policy for the apparently hard data of social science or the common sense of judicial interpretation of social life. A competing cultural interpretation challenges the authority of this interpretation of social common sense.

There is the danger that attempts to regulate through traditional legal doctrines may reproduce the victim blaming implicit in the paternalistic interpretation of the case of *Charles of the Ritz*. Naomi Wolf is careful to argue that it is lack of choice rather than the weakness of women which concerns her but it is all too easy to slip into a voice which constructs women and men as passive victims of the corporate system. This theme runs through several unconscionability decisions in Canada in relation to fraudulent marketing of dance studio lessons where individuals are induced to purchase long term contracts for unrealistic numbers of lessons. The courts do strike down the contracts, but the female consumers are constructed as "incredibly gullible", "lonely and foolish" and clearly less rational than the average consumer. It is as if the patriarchal paternalism of the law is necessary to protect naive individuals who have little ability to protect themselves in the Hobbesian world of the market.[46] This is the dark side of paternalism.

The above discussion suggests that there is no simple formula for the regulation of advertising images but that there is no reason why the law could not adopt a differing vocabulary for thinking about issues traditionally viewed through the lens of the rational and credulous. The interpretive cultural approach can also provide a rich cultural context of interpretation locating advertising images both against the background of dominant cultural assumptions and within the economic context of differing "systems of provision", *e.g.* the food or clothing system.[47] There remains the lingering question, of course, whether the law of the state is likely to be a useful resource for challenging cultural assumptions.

The conflict between the standard of the reasonable and the credulous consumer does represent ideological differences about the values and objectives of consumer protection. I indicated that over the past two decades the standard of the reasonable or credulous consumer has been an important focus for debates over the role of consumer protection in the U.S. and Europe. The standard of the reasonable consumer, developed by the Federal Trade Commission in 1983, was formulated under the influence of neo-classical economists and free market ideology. Economists argued that the protection of a few gullible people will result in lower levels of market information and/or higher costs for advertisers. There is little empirical evidence to substantiate this hypothesis. Moreover, given the elasticity of a standard such as the reasonable consumer, there is likely to remain significant uncertainty as to the application of the standard. Social science evidence is unlikely to lead to a conclusive determination. Indeed some commentators argue that it is difficult to determine whether the changed formulation

---

[46] See the discussion of these cases in J. Abramcyzk, "The Tyranny of the Majority: Liberalism in Legal Education" (1992) *Canadian Journal of Women and the Law* 442 and I. Ramsay, "Consumer law and Structures of thought: A Comment" *op. cit.*

[47] See B. Fine, "From Political Economy to Consumption" in D. Miller, ed. *Acknowledging Consumption* (1995), p. 142.

has had a direct impact on agency decisionmaking, with one author suggesting that the only difference is that it "has a different flavour than the original".[48] So does the choice of standard matter, if it is only a question of flavour?

Determining whether the standard of deception should be that of protection of the reasonable or credulous consumer is a political battle over whose vision of market relations will be made to stick in society. It is about whether to view the law as fostering relationships of trust and interdependence or as promoting a Hobbesian world of self-interested distrust. Law, through its images of social behaviour, affects the moral order of markets. It invites us, like the advertisement, to buy into and reproduce the legal images of behaviour. If the law repeatedly produces images of the consumer as a rational person, carefully weighing alternatives, then those who are taken advantage of may simply blame themselves for their failures in the marketplace.

A more appropriate understanding of a credulous person test is the assumption that consumers are entitled to trust sellers and manu-facturers. Fostering trust focuses on the sales practices used in a market and the rationale for protection is the reinforcement of trust rather than protection for the weak. Traditionally the private law of contract has been viewed as playing a limited role in fostering co-operation and trust so that one only had oneself to blame if one did not take care to fully inform oneself of the nature of a prospective transaction. Consumer protection norms were an exception to this norm and the initial development of the credulous person standard could be viewed as a critique of these contract norms. But there is increasing recognition by private law of the importance of norms of cooperation and trust in many commercial markets. The growth of the concept of good faith[49] and the development of fiduciary obligations in commercial settings are examples of these trends. The Supreme Court of Canada has recently extended the fiduciary principle to protect those middle and upper middle class individuals seeking investment advice, adverting to the importance of stimulating trust and confidence in these markets.[50] In this type of market the courts do not stress the gullibility of victims (in the particular case the plaintiff was a male stockbroker) but rather the

[48] M. Greenfield, *Consumer Law: A Guide for Those Who Represent Sellers, Lenders and Consumers* (1995), p. 179.
[49] See, *e.g.* Collins, *Good Faith, op. cit.*
[50] *Hodgkinson v. Simms* [1994] 3 S.C.R. 377.

policy of fostering trust in the market. There is much evidence that in many commercial markets norms of trust and co-operation are often central to continuing market relations and these relations fit closely the pattern of the supposedly exceptional model of fiduciary relations.[51]

It would be ironic if consumer protection policy was to embrace the reasonable consumer or the well-informed consumer as the norm, while regulators of markets dominated by white middle-class males, such as the securities markets, adopted higher levels of consumer protection. But the rejection of the trusting consumer test in misleading advertising law reflects such a trend. In Canada, consumers are currently perceived by the courts to be so smart that they will not be fooled by small print[52] or ambiguous claims and they only have themselves to blame if they are fooled. This seems to track the post-modern vision of the active consumer, unshackled from paternalistic governments, who enjoys the resistive pleasure of playing games in the market.

These ideological questions of contrasting visions of consumers and consumer markets are highlighted in the next section which discusses the remarkable rise of the constitutional doctrine of commercial speech.

2 Commercial Speech: the New Constitution of the Market

A central chapter in the dominant narrative of advertising is the development of the doctrine of commercial speech in relation to corporate advertising. This doctrine reflects a U.S. cultural transplant which has had a significant instrumental and ideological impact on regulation of advertising in North America and Europe. It is linked to the resurgence of neo-classical economic arguments of advertising as information and ideologies of the free market. An example of its impact on regulators is the statement by senior officials at the U.S. Federal Trade Commission that, "both the commercial speech doctrine and

---

[51] See R. Gordon, "Unfreezing Legal Reality: Critical Approaches to Law" (1987) 15 *University of Florida L. Rev.* 195 at 207.
[52] See, *e.g. R. v. International Vacations Ltd* (1980) 33 O.R. (2d) 327 Blair J. at 332 (Ontario Court of Appeal) "the average reader ... literate, intelligent and unlikely to make a relatively large monetary commitment without carefully reading the advertisement".

the FTCs consumer protection policy are founded on a free market rationale".[53]

In 1916 the Supreme Court of the United States characterised advertising as basic information about a product, commenting, somewhat dismissively, that "advertising is merely identification and description, apprising of quality and price. It has no other object than to draw attention to the article to be sold ..."[54] This prompted a criticism in the *Journal of Political Economy* of the court's ignorance of developments in merchandising techniques:

> "Has the judge never delved in to the new business of advertising? Does he not know of the eager study of the methods of appeal, of the principles of psychology, of art, of colour effects, of design, of the power of words? ... There is no place for the educational advertising campaign, the development of new wants."[55]

Sixty years later the Supreme Court, in *Virginia State Board of Pharmacy v. Virginia Citizens Consumer Council*,[56] described advertising as information, but the importance of this informational function was to transform "speech which does 'no more than propose a commercial transaction'[57]" into a form of constitutionally protected speech, establishing a precedent, since adopted internationally, for the doctrine of commercial speech. In this case, public interest consumer and labour groups had challenged prohibitions on price advertising for prescription drugs by licensed pharmacists in Virginia. In striking down the restriction as a contravention of the First Amendment Blackmun J., speaking for the majority, indicated that advertising could be regarded as falling within traditional rationales for the protection of speech under the First Amendment, in particular that of furthering the marketplace of ideas in society. Moreover:

> "Advertising, however tasteless and excessive it sometimes may seem, is nonetheless dissemination of information as to who is producing and selling

---

[53] C. Lee Peeler and Michelle K. Rusk, "Commercial Speech and the FTCs Consumer Protection Program" (1991) 59 *Antitrust Law Journal* 985.

[54] *Rast v. van Deman & Lewis* 240 U.S. 342 (1916).

[55] C. Duncan, "The Economics and Legality of Premium Giving" 24 *Journal of Political Economy* 928 at 947 quoted in S. Strasser, *Satisfaction Guaranteed: The making of the American Market* (1989), p. 178.

[56] 425 U.S. 748 (1976).

[57] Blackmun J. at 762 citing to *Pittsburgh Press Co. v. Human Relations Commission* 413 U.S. 376 (1973) at 385.

what product, for what reason, and at what price. So long as we preserve a predominantly free enterprise economy, the allocation of our resources in large measure will be made through numerous private economic decisions. It is a matter of public interest that those decisions, in the aggregate, be intelligent and well informed. To this end the free flow of commercial information is indispensable".[58]

Blackmun J. also argued that there was a "listener's right to receive advertising" and characterised the existing restrictions as a "highly paternalistic" limitation on the free flow of information to consumers who would be capable of perceiving their own interests if they were provided with adequate information.

Rehnquist J., in dissent, rejected the elevation of advertising to constitutional protection. In his view, the decision of the majority was a resurrection of the approach taken by the court in pre-New Deal decisions, where it had treated existing market relations as natural and pre-political institutions, and regulation, such as minimum wage laws, as unjustifiable interferences with property rights of employers. This approach embedded a particular, but contingent, set of market ground rules as beyond alteration by the democratic process. Rehnquist J. saw a similar consequence with the adoption of commercial speech and commented that "there is certainly nothing in the United States Constitution which requires the Virginia legislature to hew to the teachings of Adam Smith" and scoffed at the idea of the First Amendment applying to "a 'merchant' who goes from door-to-door selling pots".[59] As for the argument that advertising helped to enlighten public decision-making he stated: "I had understood this view to relate to public decision making as to political, social and other public issue, rather than the decision of a particular individual as to whether to purchase one or another kind of shampoo."[60]

A later decision of the Supreme Court of Canada which imported the doctrine to Canada summarised the rationales for constitutional protection of commercial speech as based not only on the welfare enhancing argument of informed economic choices but also the rationale that market choices were "an important aspect of individual self fulfilment and personal autonomy".[61]

---

[58] Blackmun J. at 765.
[59] Rehnquist J. at 782 and 786.
[60] *ibid.*, at 786.
[61] *Ford v. AG Quebec* [1988] 2 S.C.R. 712, (1989) 54 D.L.R. (4th.) 577 at 618.

The majority decision in *Virginia Pharmacy* reflected motives of distributive justice since the suppression of prescription drug price information disadvantaged mostly the poor, the sick and the aged. It was an action brought by public interest consumer groups and an important rationale for protection was consumer rights to information, with the ban on advertising restricting those rights. The irony is that while the commercial speech doctrine was forged to further social justice, many commentators now see it as having been harnessed to a corporate agenda of deregulation, foreshadowing a corporate cultural hegemony over markets in North America and Europe.[62] It is difficult to measure the influence of this doctrine on public policy but it has become an important bargaining weapon used by the commercial media, corporate, and advertising groups to attack regulation, particularly in such areas as the advertising of tobacco[63] and alcohol and advertising to children. Its symbolic significance is enhanced because large advertisers are often in a favourable position to produce popular reproductions of the doctrine, shorn of legal nuances and complexities, in various media. The doctrine has seeped into popular discourse in the media and non-legal journals so that one hears talk of a constitutional "right to advertise".

There are certain recurring patterns of thought in decisions on commercial speech. There is the distinction between the free flow of information (the free market) and regulation. While regulation of advertising may be justified to ensure a clean flow (*e.g.* through proscription of misleading information), this will still be an *intervention* into the market. A note in the *Harvard Law Review* summarises this viewpoint, indicating that regulation of advertising reflects the tension between "the value of the free circulation of commercial information and the value of consumer protection against harmful commercial speech".[64] In addition, there is the contrast between paternalism and autonomy with bans and restrictions on advertising viewed as interferences with individual autonomy, representing attempts "to manipu-

[62] See for example F. Schauer, "The political incidence of the Free Speech doctrine" (1993) 64 *Univ. Colorado L. Rev.* 635: C. Sunstein, "Free Speech Now" (1992) 59 *Univeristy of Chicago Legal Forum* 255: A. Hutchinson, "Money Talk: Against Constitutionalizing (Commercial) Speech (1990) *Canadian Business Law Journal* 2: O. Fiss, "Free Speech and Social Structure" (1986) 71 *Iowa L. Rev.* 1405.
[63] See *RJR Macdonald v. Canada (Attorney–General)* [1995] 3 S.C.R. 199.
[64] "The Supreme Court-Leading Cases" (1986) 100 *Harv. L.R.* 100 at 172.

late private behaviour by depriving citizens of truthful information concerning lawful activities".[65]

This structure of thought is similar to the approach of the European Court of Justice to issues of consumer standards as non-tariff barriers to trade under article 30 of the E.C. Treaty. Since the decision in *Cassis de Dijon*[66] the approach of the court has been to view consumer protection standards as a limitation on the free circulation of goods within the Community, and justified only if they are proportionate to an identifiable market failure. The political objective of the court has until recently,[67] been deregulatory, and it is assumed, though not proved, that this politics has provided consumers with greater choice in goods and services. There is replicated here the concept of free choice versus protection with underlying themes of freedom versus paternalism. There is, therefore, a similar structure of thought in relation to both the commercial market for goods and the commercial market of ideas.

These distinctions mirror almost exactly the U.S. pre-New deal approach to economic regulation by government. Government action was viewed as intervention in a pre-political sphere of "free" market activity. The achievement of writers such as Robert Hale[68] was to explode this structure of thought by pointing out that all markets are the creatures of law and that the common law of contract, tort and property, with their elaborate rules of permission and prohibition were simply another form of government regulation, backed up by state force. The ground rules of markets would therefore have significant distributional impact on the power of market actors. An unregulated market did not imply a vacuum of power or that legal structures were necessarily neutral. To deny this reality was to indulge in ideological mystification and privilege a particular form of market relations.

The same criticism may be levelled at much judicial rhetoric around advertising and commercial speech. Cultural studies adds a further

---

[65] *Posadas de Puerto Rico Associates v. Tourism Company of Puerto Rico* 478 U.S. 328, 106 S.Ct. 2968. Breman J. dissenting at 350 (1986).
[66] [1979] E.C.R. 649.
[67] Recent cases suggest a drawing back from this approach. See N. Reich, "The November Revolution of the European Court of Justice: *Keck, Meng* and *Audi* Revisited" (1994) 31 C.M.L.R. 459.
[68] See R. Hale. "Coercion and Distribution in a Supposedly non-coercive state" (1923) 38 *Political Science Quarterly* 470; "Bargaining, Duress and Economic Liberty" (1943) *Columbia L. Rev.* 603.

aspect to the realist critique. The ground rules of markets in consumer capitalism may not merely allocate economic bargaining power. They also affect the potential cultural influence of these markets in shaping consciousness, for example, in relation to specific issues such as sex-role stereotyping and images of minorities, or the extent to which there is a pervasive "White Noise" of commercialism to everyday life. The approach to commercial advertising as merely market information neglects the reality of this inevitable mixture of economy and culture in most contemporary advertising.

The constitutional protection of advertising is justified often by the metaphorical marketplace of ideas rationale for protection of freedom of expression. Classical writers on freedom of expression assumed that in this competition for ideas, truth would ultimately succeed. But many writers argue that in the consumer capitalism of the late twentieth century the marketplace of ideas bears little resemblance to a level playing field. Just as there are market failures in the marketplace for goods, so there are failures in the competitive conditions of the marketplace of ideas. Substantiation for this thesis is found in the growth of "culture trusts", large scale media conglomerates which dominate the communications system. The implications of the commercial dominance of U.S. media for the style and content of programming in the USA has been well documented. Networks sell audiences to advertisers and advertisers have significant direct and indirect control over programming. They are entitled to preview programmes for "suitability".[69] Proctor and Gamble require that programming should avoid portraying business as "cold ruthless, and lacking all sentiments or spiritual motivation" and that it should not attack "some basic conception of the American way of life".[70] Advertisers avoid controversial programming and most programmes which raise social issues generally convert them into personal problems to be addressed at the family or individual level, with facile endings. Groups which are not of market interest, such as low income consumers, will find little material which reflects issues which affect them in their daily

---

[69] See, e.g. J. Blumler "Television in the United States: Funding Sources and Programming Consequences" in West Yorkshire Media Politics Group, *Research on the Range and Quality of Broadcasting Services; A Report for the Committee on Financing of the BBC* (1986) and see generally E. Baker, *Democracy and Freedom of Expression* (1993). Blumler notes that there is a co-operative screening company formed by major ad agencies which previews programmes for compatibility with the advertisers "programme content sensitivies".

[70] E. Herman, "The Market Attack on Dissent" *Z Magazine* (March 1996), at 53.

life. One commentator notes the irony of the existence of these controls by advertisers in a society so committed to the First Amendment and wonders why "a society which safeguards the sanctity of communication from possible invasion by certain political interests should generate no indignation over equivalent inroads from a different source".[71]

Other writers point to the large growth in advocacy advertising (where corporations portray the generally beneficial role which the company or free enterprise plays within the community) and communications strategies by business since the early 1970s,[72] the increasing corporate sponsorship of all forms of sports and culture and the denial of access to the commercial media for critical consumer commentary on business practices.[73] The idea that truth has a natural advantage in the marketplace of ideas seems "fragile"[74] in the world of contemporary public relations and marketing. Cumulatively these factors suggest that the marketplace of ideas has become more like a shopping mall of identities and lifestyles. But it is a shopping mall where many voices are marginalised or excluded. Both the images and reality of the lives of poor people and minorities are often excluded: the images, because they are not perceived to be a market, and the reality through spatial segregation. Moreover, individuals are significantly constrained in putting forward alternative ideas through the high costs of obtaining access to the media. Attempts to exercise freedom of speech to critique corporate culture will often hit the brick wall of the law of copyright and trademarks, and defamation remains a significant threat to alternative discourses.

The above is not intended to reflect a conspiracy theory of the media and corporate power. But it is extremely important to acknowledge that just as an unregulated market does not imply an absence of economic power so unregulated commercial speech does not necessarily lead to "the free flow" of information. It suggests that there may be a need for government to prevent the detrimental consequences for public life of a culture dominated by corporate voices. In a similar vein, the European Court of Justice, with its deregulatory politics, is not creating a "free market" but a new set of ground rules which may, for example,

---

[71] Blumler *op. cit.*, at 123.
[72] See J. Nelson, *Sultans of Sleaze* (1989).
[73] See discussion in E. Baker, *Advertising and a Democratic Press* (1994).
[74] Schauer, *op. cit.*, p. 953.

favour larger over smaller units of capital and may or may not increase consumer choice in the long run.[75]

Defenders of commercial speech argue that the courts are able to distinguish the different roles of advertising and can separate the beneficial informational role of advertising which deserves protection, from other manipulative and persuasive aspects.[76] This may appear like a pragmatic balancing of interests but there are three concerns with this position. First, it is simply not clear that the rationales for protection of freedom of expression embrace commercial advertising. Secondly, the courts lack a sophisticated theory of the cultural role of advertising. Thirdly, although the courts may draw legal distinctions between different types of advertising, the fact that advertising is prima facie protected speech means that it is this aspect which will be stressed by the media rather than the more nuanced legal version. It is this version which will become sedimented in common sense.

The recognition by the law of commercial speech has two ideological consequences. It acts as a buffer to regulation while disguising the contrived nature of the existing market and the role of advertising in shaping the contours of the market. By assuming that only government is a distorter of some natural market realm, it also permits a critique of existing regulations in terms of abstract ideas of freedom and autonomy. Bans become "censorship" in popular discourse, part of the "nanny state". It is unlikely that many individuals are convinced by this rhetoric in relation to products such as tobacco, but commercial speech may still be a powerful advance guard in the extension of consumer capitalism.

Even at an abstract level, the rationales for protection of commercial speech seem thin. There is undoubtedly an informational role to advertising, and restrictions on advertising in certain professional markets may reduce consumer welfare. This provides an appropriate rationale for economic deregulation but hardly an argument for con- stitutional protection. The listener's right to information seems a more plausible argument for the protection of commercial speech. Perhaps

---

[75] For an argument that deregulation may not increase choice see H.C. von Heyderbrand u.d. Lasa, "Free movement of Foodstuffs, Consumer Protection and Food Standards in the European Community: Has the Court of Justice Got it Wrong?" (1991) 16 E.L.R. 391.

[76] See R. Sharpe, "Commercial Expression and the Charter" (1987) 37 *University of Toronto Law Journal* 299.

it is a harbinger of consumer rights as human rights.[77] Understood in the Hohfeldian sense such a right would imply a correlative duty to provide information, and this is recognised in many aspects of consumer law, such as truth in lending, labelling laws and so on. Most of these rights grew out of the need to protect consumers against abuses of bargaining power by business corporations and might be classified as forms of economic or social rights which are often dependent on state "intervention". Taking seriously a consumer's right to information would result in much higher levels of corporate disclosure than exist currently. One could imagine new car dealers being required to provide consumers with a detailed prospectus similar to the disclosures under U.S. securities legislation. It seems odd to view advertising, which is a particularly one sided form of communication as satisfying any such right to information.

A final argument for protection is based, not on economic concerns, but on the right to autonomy and self-fulfilment which is thought to be achieved through informed economic choices. This conjures up an image of "best buy" rational consumer behaviour. It is unlikely that judges putting forward this argument were thinking of Mr Overton in Chapter 2 or the advertising for cosmetics. But this form of lifestyle and image advertising dominates modern advertising so that the marketplace has become a marketplace of identities. Autonomy and self-fulfilment is promised through the continued consumption of signs, of lifestyles and identities. Advertising is interested in selling not only the particular lifestyle, but cumulatively, is selling a way of life. Constitutional protection for this form of market culture elevates a particular form of lifestyle, "the compleat consumer", to the level of a constitutional norm. Paraphrasing Rehnquist J., it hardly seems part of the liberal tradition for a constitution to endorse a particular form of life. The post-modern idea that we seek our identities through a continuous series of lifestyles, establishing meaning for our lives through the mechanism of commodity consumption is, as we have seen, a controversial thesis. It would seem odd that it should be enshrined as a constitutional norm, essentially placing much advertising beyond regulation by the democratic process.

Defenders of the doctrine argue that the courts can distinguish the

---

[77] See S. Deutsch, "Are Consumer Rights Human Rights?" (1994) Osgoode Hall L.J. 537.

differing roles of advertising in consumer markets but confidence in that judgment may be weakened by the example of the Supreme Court of Canada in its decision on the regulation of tobacco advertising. In this case, the court, by a narrow majority, struck down those sections of the *Tobacco Products Control Act* which banned tobacco advertising and which required tobacco companies to post unattributed health warnings on cigarette packages.[78] The strength of the ideology of advertising as information is reflected in the majority decision of the court which was based on the argument that the ban on advertising did not minimally impair the right to freedom of expression.[79] The government failed to demonstrate that less intrusive regulation, such as bans on lifestyle advertising or advertising to children, would not have achieved the objective of reducing cigarette consumption. The ban denied information on brand preference and content to existing consumers of tobacco products who might use this information to reduce their risk to health.

Mclachlin J., who delivered the majority judgment, commented that "[the] advertising ban deprives those who lawfully choose to smoke of information relating to price, quality and even health risks associated with different brands." Her judgment seemed remarkably formalistic in its ideological attachment to the importance of advertising as information. She treated as similar phenomena tobacco advertising by large multinational corporations using sophisticated psychological marketing, and advertising by dentists of the price of their services. The focus on providing information on rational choice seemed curious given the addictive nature of tobacco consumption. Her inability to understand the symbolic use of brand images as a method of creating a favourable image for a product and potentially increasing consumption is evident in her approach to the use of tobacco product logos on articles such as tobacco lighters. She comments that "it is hard to imagine how the presence of a tobacco logo on a cigarette lighter, for example, would increase consumption".[80]

In contrast, the minority judgment concluded that the ban was justified after an analysis of the nature of tobacco advertising and the

[78] *RJR MacDonald v. A-G Canada* [1995] 3 S.C.R. 199.
[79] See below p. 109 in the discussion of *Irwin Toy v. Attorney General of Quebec* a description of the concept of minimal impairment in the context of the Canadian Charter of Rights and Freedoms.
[80] Mclachlin J. at 342.

uncertainties of social science evidence concerning the relation between advertising bans and consumption. La Forest J., delivering the minority judgment, related tobacco advertising to traditional rationales for protection of freedom of expression, namely the search for truth, the protection of individual autonomy and self-development and the promotion of public participation in the democratic process. He concluded that it was as far from the core of these values as soliciting for the purpose of prostitution, hate mongering or pornography. "[I]ts sole purpose is to inform consumers about, and promote the use of, a product that is harmful, and often fatal, to the consumers who use it."[81]

He described the sophisticated tobacco advertisement campaigns, using "the most advanced advertising and social psychology techniques", and concluded that this undermined "their claim to freedom of expression protection because it creates an enormous power differential between these companies and tobacco consumers in the marketplace of ideas."[82] He described in detail internal advertising documents of the tobacco companies commenting that "although the appellants steadfastly argue that their marketing efforts are directed solely at maintaining and expanding brand loyalty among adult smokers their documents show otherwise."[83]

In his opinion the tobacco companies had developed advocacy thrusts to reassure existing consumers and associate their product with an attractive lifestyle, particularly to the young and non-smokers. Advertising reinforced "the social acceptability of smoking by identifying it with glamour, affluence, youthfulness and vitality". In one internal tobacco document of 1987, reference is made under the title "Whose Behaviour are We trying to affect" to "18–34; Emphasis 18–24 (new users)" and to "High School—some post secondary education". It continues "Psychographics":

> "Young adults who are currently in the process of establishing their independence and their position in society. They look for peer group acceptance in their brand selection ... As young adults they look for symbols that will help to reinforce their independence and individuality".[84]

The marketing documents in this case reveal the standard form of

---

[81] La Forest J. at 283.
[82] ibid.
[83] ibid., at 285.
[84] ibid., at 298.

sophisticated product marketing and lifestyle advertising used in many sectors. It is part of the private sociology of consumer behaviour maintained by corporate organisations selling to consumers. Breakfast cereal manufacturers use psychographics and collect vast amounts of data on their potential consumers. These data surface rarely in the public domain. What is of concern is their use in relation to a harmful product and the sharp contrast with the idea of advertising as information. Indeed the logic of the minority judgment was that tobacco advertising deserved no constitutional protection under freedom of expression, rather than the conclusion in fact reached which upheld government regulation of this form of speech.

The majority and minority judgments reveal again the dichotomy between advertising as information and advertising as manipulation. There was no reference to literature from cultural studies in developing the manipulation argument. The minority does not provide guidance beyond the harmful nature of the product, as to why the practices of the tobacco companies should be regulated. Since most corporations use similar marketing techniques in selling to consumers it could be argued that there is a general imbalance in consumer markets between producers and consumers in relation to the market for ideas. A cultural approach could have strengthened the argument for prohibition by pointing out that even if there was not clear social science evidence as to the effects of advertising on consumption, the secondary message of the advertisements, associating tobacco smoking with favourable social images, was a harmful practice. It could have also underlined the difficulty, outlined by the minority, in separating information from image in advertising. The majority had conceded that the government could have banned lifestyle advertising. But the development of the "this-is-not-an-ad" approach described in Chapter 3 indicates the ability of advertisers to use apparently contentless messages to create a distinctive brand image.

A basic question remains whether there are good reasons for any constitutional protection of advertising. The free speech tradition in the USA[85] was forged to protect minorities against harassment by the state but seems to have become a weapon of the powerful in the private sector. Classical writers on speech had viewed the commercial media as the enemy of an enlightened democracy because it did not cultivate

---

[85] See C. Sunstein, "Free Speech Now" (1992) *University of Chicago Legal Forum* 255.

"those qualities of taste, or reasoned judgment ... of mutual understanding upon which the enterprise of self-government depends. On
the contrary it is a mighty force for breaking them down. It corrupts
both our morals and our intelligence."[86] While we might detect an
intellectual distaste for popular culture in this comment, there remains
the important political question of the control of the marketplace of
ideas by a concentrated commercial media. Advertisers are not a
minority voice, nor do they speak on behalf of minorities. The doctrine
is not necessary as a method of consumer protection which can be
achieved generally by direct measures through the legislature. Consumers remain a voice with some influence in the democratic process
and are able to pursue their rights to information through the legislative
process.

The idea of commercial speech does not have such a hold over the
European imagination as in the United States, although it has been
tentatively recognised in decisions under the European Convention on
Human Rights. The increasing deregulation of the media in many
countries means that similar issues concerning commercial influence
over media and markets will be exposed.[87] The doctrine of commercial
speech is ultimately anti-democratic since it removes from democratic
control the regulation of market behaviour and allows corporations to
establish the ground rules of consumer markets. It has little connection
with traditional rationales for free speech. While government has
traditionally been viewed as the enemy of free speech a major threat
to autonomy and self-fulfilment may be posed by the con-
stitutionalisation of corporate speech.

3 The limits of consumer culture? Capitalism, Advertising to Children and the First Amendment

The regulation of advertising to children appears to be an important
limiting case on the "consumerisation" of social life. Childhood is
regarded by many as a special aspect of an individual's development,
and a central criticism of advertising to children has been that children

---

[86] A. Meiklejohn, *Free Speech and its Relation to Government* (1948), p. 104.
[87] For evidence of these concerns see T. Gibbons, *op. cit.*, Chap. 6.

should not be treated as "miniature consumers".[88] It might be thought, therefore, that regulation of advertising to children is a special case of a vulnerable audience, an exceptional situation requiring a special response. While there is some truth in this perspective, an examination of the competing arguments and assumptions over advertising to children highlights more general questions concerning the cultural effects of advertising.

Regulation of advertising to children raises overlapping questions of social science (measurement of harm to children), political ideology (the relative role of parents and the state in regulating children's behaviour), and cultural assumptions about childhood and the values of consumer capitalism. Charting the mixture of these issues in the development of policy illuminates more general questions about understanding the power of advertising in society.

There is a relatively long history of concern over the impact of advertising on children in North America,[89] where the regulation of advertising to children has been a recurring topic on the public policy agenda since the late 60s.[90] The debates over regulation have often

---

[88] The influential U.S. pressure group Action for Children's Television in their first News Release in 1969 stressed that "children were special human beings, not miniature consumers". Action for Children's Television, News Release September 1969.

[89] See F. Wartella and B. Reeves, "Historical Trends in Research on Children and the Media 1900–1960" (1985) *Journal of Communications* 109.

[90] A useful account of Federal Trade Commission involvement in this area until 1976 may be found in G. Thain, "Suffer the Hucksters to Come Unto the Little Children? Possible Restrictions of Television Advertising to Children under Section 5 of the Federal Trade Commission Act" (1976) 56 *Boston University Law Review* 651 at 656–664. The Final Staff Report of the Commission in 1981 summarises at pp. 5–15 the development of regulation of advertising to children by the Commission. See Federal Trade Commission *In the Matter of Children's Advertising: Final Staff Report and Recommendations* (March, 1981). The controversial rulemaking proceedings of the late 70s is discussed from differing perspectives in M. Pertschuk *Revolt against Regulation* (1982), Chap. 6 and Bernice R. Hasin *Consumers Commission and Congress: Law Theory and the Federal Trade Commission, 1968–85* (1987) and see R. Mnookin and Susan Bartlett-Foote "The Kidvid Crusade", (1980) *Public Interest* 94. A valuable analysis of the ideological issues around consumer regulation at this time is R. Harris and S. Milkis *The Politics of Regulatory Change: a tale of two agencies* (1990), Chap. 5 especially at pp. 154–186. During the 1980s the Commission, apart from bringing an occasional action against an individual advertiser showed no interest in this area. There appears to be a greater interest now in the general topic of advertising to children.

A useful outline of the history in Canada until 1982 is found in M. Goldberg, "TV Advertising Directed at children: Inherently Unfair or Simply in Need of Regulation?" in *Marketplace Canada: Some Controversial Dimensions* (S. Shapiro and L. Heslop, eds. 1982) Chap. 1.

The early history of the development of the movement for abolition in Quebec from

been remarkably heated and generated extensive interest. When the Federal Communications Commission invited comments from the public in 1970 on a proposed rulemaking on the related topic of children's television it received over 100,000 comments and the public record consisted of 63 volumes of comments and letters, almost overwhelmingly critical of children's television.

The Federal Trade Commission initiated hearings in the late 1970s to determine whether advertising to children should be banned.[91] These hearings became a focus for a massive attack on the Commission by advertisers, broadcasters and industry associations. A consortium of lobbyists raised "a war chest" of $16,000,000 to fight the rule which was constructed as a symbol of meddlesome "social engineering"[92] by government bureaucracies. In a highly significant editorial the "Washington Post" described the Commission as a "National Nanny",[93] proposing to substitute governmental for parental authority. The rulemaking was ultimately terminated in 1981, the Commission's powers were curtailed by Congress and the Commission was reshaped in the image of Reaganism and neo-classical economics. Controversy continues, however, over the commercialisation of programming to children. More recent issues include the use of programme length commercials and character merchandising,[94] the insinuation of advertising into school programmes,[95] and the marketing of cigarettes to children. In 1990 the U.S. Congress enacted legislation addressing the

---

1969–73 is documented in G. Larose *Le Mouvement pour l'abolition de la publicité destinée aux enfants* (Masters Thesis, Université de Montreal 1973).

The movement towards "Television Without Frontiers" in Europe coupled with deregulatory pressures from broadcasters and advertisers now appears to raise in Europe similar issues to those discussed in the USA and Canada. In the U.K. the movement towards greater commercialisation of the media has raised questions about the commercialisation of children's broadcasting.

[91] The Staff Report which initiated the rulemaking is E. Ratner, J. Hellegers, Stern G. *Federal Trade Commission Staff Report on Television Advertising to Children* (1978).

[92] The most famous symbol of this attack was the Washington Post editorial of March 1, 1978 which described the Commission's initiative in Children advertising under the headline "The FTC as National Nanny".

[93] Washington Post, March 1, 1978.

[94] See discussion in T. Englehart, "The Shortcake Strategy" in *Watching Television* (1986) T. Gitlin ed.

[95] See "The Nation" (November 1992). The debate has focused on Whittle communications which offers free video and news programmes to schools on condition that they show two minutes of advertising time.

issue of commercialism on Children Television.[96] The *New York Times* periodically publishes editorial comments on the problems of commercial advertising to children and *Newsweek* has described network "kidvid" as "a national embarrassment ... a brain rotting assault of animated comic books and shrieking commercials that borders on child abuse".[97] Tom Englehart describes these recurring debates over the impact of media and advertising on children as "a periodic frenzy".[98] The growing commercialisation of children's television in Europe in recent years has led to the emergence of similar concerns and the North American experience may shed light on these debates.[99]

The use of children in selling mass-produced products dates back to the nineteenth century, and there had been concerns in the 1930s about the impact of radio advertising on children's educational development. The large growth of network television advertising to children during the 1960s in the USA and Canada stimulated concern among public interest groups and caught the attention of regulators. Analysis of advertising and business trade publications of the 1960s reveals a realisation of the importance of children both as a market and as a means of selling to adults.[1] For example, writing in 1962 in *Printers' Ink* the vice president of Grey Advertising whose accounts included a number of toy companies, peanut butter and chocolate companies described how he revived the market share of Ward's snacks by directing its advertisements to children rather than adults.

---

[96] Pub. L. No. 101–437. This Act requires the Federal Communications Commission to reintroduce commercial guidelines for children's programming and to initiate a rulemaking proceeding on the issue of commercial content in children's programming. Advertising must not exceed 10.5 minutes per hour on weekends and not more than 12 minutes during the weekday. In Canada outside Quebec the current limit is eight minutes per hour. The U.S. legislation is less stringent than the FCC guidelines of 1974 which had limited advertisements to nine and a half minutes/hour on weekends and 12 minutes during weekdays. In 1986 the FCC had deregulated children's television, removing commercial guidelines on the theory that the market would police excessive advertising. This decision was successfully challenged by Action for Children's Television. See *Action for Children Television v. FCC* 821 F.2d. 741 (1987). A useful summary of the history of FCC involvement in this area may be found in "Broadcast Regulation, Has the Marketplace Failed the Children: The Children's Television Act of 1990" 15 *Seton Hall Legislative Journal* 345 (1991).

[97] *Newsweek* (January 8, 1990).

[98] Englehart, *op. cit.*, p. 110.

[99] See Advertising Standards Authority, *Monthly Report* No. 37 (June 15, 1994) describing an ASA seminar of advertising to children.

[1] I am indebted to Didi Herman for these data.

"There had to be a reason to make the housewife pick Ward's so we decided her kids could make up her mind for her ... Once we could get the kids yelling for the cakes we knew that mom would go along. So we got up a complete advertising, marketing, merchandising and publicity campaign directed at them and ignoring adults. We even redesigned the package for them."[2]

The medium chosen for reaching children was television. "Once agreement was reached that youngsters were to be the target the medium picked to reach them quickly was TV—the TV spot."[3]

Television was a powerful medium for selling to children and William Melody has described how the development of children's TV[4] in the USA followed the pattern of U.S. television financing, namely the sales of audiences to advertisers. In the early 1950s there were a number of quality children's television programmes as part of a campaign to increase television ownership. The shift to mass audience programming in the late 1950s led to the downgrading of children's TV and the creation of the Saturday morning "ghetto". The early shows by Disney had been expensive and in 1958 Hanna Barbara sold their first low cost cartoon to Kelloggs which at this time syndicated programmes. Saturday morning programming became a clustering of low-cost cartoons surrounded by advertising for toys, cereals, snack foods and sweets and the virtual lack of separation of programming from advertising.

Network children's television in the USA continues to represent the

---

[2] *Printers' Ink* (November 9, 1962).
[3] *Sales Management* Vol 96 (February 18, 1966). In describing the youth market in 1963 it is stated that it divides into three distinct marketing segments: elementary school pupils, high schoolers and college students (*Printers' Ink*, 1963 p. 284). In 1966 there is described a special unit in an advertising agency entitled "Children Marketing Opportunity" which helps producers reach the child market without making any basic change in existing products or investing in new manufacturing facilities. "We will take an existing product and aim it at kids by creating a new child oriented name, label, package and ad campaign".

In 1970 Walter Margulies wrote in 41 *Advertising Age* 90 that: "one vital segment of that younger half of our population still appears to be underestimated, misunderstood, and generally neglected: the nearly 55,000,000 children under the age of 12. Who cares about a consumer with a weekly income of 50c? True, even if that mini-consumer spent as much as nickel a week on your product it would only amount to $2.60 a year. But how profits would soar if you could capture some 10,000,000 or 20,000,000 of those tykes as regular weekly customers.

Of course, even more important than children's personal expenditures are their enormous influences on parents buying decisions..."
[4] See W. Melody *The Economics of Exploitation* (1973).

most extreme form of the basic commercial logic of U.S. television with the resulting uniformity of content in its offerings. In a review of the financing of U.S. television in 1986, Jay Blumler outlined the offerings of the three networks on Saturday December 14th, 1985[5] and, apart from noting the standardisation of format and style, commented that the "commercialization of children's programs, including close ties between leading characters and toys on sales in the shops, is ... extraordinary blatant ... One can understand why several of our most critical informants condemned this pattern as "criminal".[6]

In Canada the greater presence of public broadcasting may lessen some of the critical bite of this comment but many children watch U.S. programming and a survey showed that 85 per cent of children's programming by private stations in Toronto (the largest market) were animated cartoons, most programming was made in the USA and the writers concluded that children were being provided with little variety with television stations being content to "follow the market".[7] The recent growth of cable and speciality channels might promise a reduction in advertising, and an increase in choice, but they remain generally highly commercialised in terms of product tie-ins to the characters on the programmes.

The major criticism of advertising to children is that it is inherently unfair for the powerful and pervasive media to exploit the vulnerable child for commercial gain and to insinuate consumerist values into childhood. This is often supported by alarming statistics concerning the number of hours of advertising which the average child would be exposed to throughout their childhood. The Federal Trade Commission began its report in 1978 with the statement that "[i]n 1977, the average American child aged two through 11 was exposed to more than 20,000 television commercials".[8] In addition to this general critique of the commercialisation of children's media several specific criticisms recur. First, children should not be used as surrogate sales persons to pester their parents to buy advertised products. This could lead to unnecessary family conflicts and make the burden of parenting even harder for the

[5] See J.G. Blumler "Television in the United States: Funding Sources and Programming Consequences" in *Broadcasting Finance in Transition* (J. Blumler and T.J. Nossiter eds. 1991).
[6] *ibid.*, p. 78.
[7] A. Caron and E. van Every, *Children's Television in Canada and Europe: An Analysis of Canadian Children's Programming and Preferences* (1991) p. 25.
[8] Federal Trade Commission Staff Report, *op. cit.*, p. 13.

majority of women who shoulder the burden of family shopping. These problems were exacerbated in lower income households where children would see images of products which their parents could not afford. Some black writers in the USA view the consumerist values in kid's advertising as a form of abuse of poor black children who have, through the electronic media, immediate access to a mainstream consumer culture which promises them prestige and status through the ownership of commodities which they cannot often afford.[9] When the media reported that the motive for a young black boy being murdered by another turned out to be his designer shoes, this seemed to confirm the worst fears of the harm from commercial advertising.[10] Secondly, there were objections to specific techniques such as host selling, the use of cartoon characters such as Tony the Tiger which exploited children's trust, fast photography and premiums and the failure to separate clearly commercials from programming. Thirdly, there was concern about the nature of the products advertised on children's television (primarily pre-sweetened cereals, biscuits, toys and vitamins) which created potential health problems and raised questions about the proper norms of child development. Finally, children's advertising often relied on negative or exclusionary gender and race stereotyping. In an article in *The New York Times* in 1992 entitled "What are commercials selling to children?" the response was "A world where food is sweet, blond is best and all girls like dolls" and "blacks play supporting roles."[11]

Opponents of regulation argued that bans or severe limits on advertising would erode the economic base of children's television and prevent broadcasting of high quality programmes. (The commercial networks in the USA have not, however, been conspicuous in their production of high quality programming, with most quality pro-gramming being produced by the public broadcasting network.) Opponents also argued that bans on advertising to children would contravene the First Amendment. This argument was fortified by the development in the USA of protection for commercial speech.[12] In

---

[9] See R. Austin, "A Nation of Thieves": Securing Black Peoples Right to Shop and Sell in White America" (1994) *Utah L. Rev.* 147 at 159 citing C. Nightingale, *On the Edge: A History of Poor Black Children and their American Dreams* (1993).

[10] See R.K.L. Collins "Sneakers that Kill" 1:3 *Adbusters* noting that "in Baltimore, tennis shoes have become the motive for murder".

[11] *New York Times*, Review/Television, J. O'Connor (undated).

[12] The watershed case was *Virginia State Pharmacy Board of Pharmacy et al. v. Virginia Citizens Consumers Council Inc. et al.* 425 U.S. 748 (1976).

addition, the issue of the viewing habits of children was properly a parental responsibility and not one for the state. This was the central message of the "National Nanny" editorial. Finally, a recurring theme in industry defences of advertising to children was that children were much smarter than assumed by those who would regulate advertising and that regulation was a futile gesture since children are exposed to other commercial influences and attempting to exclude TV advertisements created an artificial environment. Advertising might in fact help to socialise children to the modern consumer society.

The debates over advertising to children raised the issue of the power of advertising and how to conceptualise and measure its impact. As public policy interest increased in the late 1960s, this stimulated social science research on the impact of advertising to children. The absence of social science evidence on the impact of advertising on children was used during the early period (late 1960s/early 1970s) as a justification for not taking regulatory action. Regulators in both Canada and the USA used the lack of data as a reason for not taking action or preferring the lighter touch of industry self-regulation. It served both as a substitute for decision-making (study it further and hope it will go away) and a legitimation for decisions reached on other grounds (a fear of interfering with the commercial financing of television).[13] Social science was appealed to as providing rational firm ground in contrast to the "emotionalism" surrounding the issue. There was more than a hint of sexism in this construction since children's advertising was viewed primarily as an issue raised by "mothers".

Social science studies during the 1970s and 1980s attempted to

---

[13] See J. Howard and J. Hulbert, *Advertising and the Public Interest: A Staff Report to the Federal Trade Commission*, (1973) p. 29. "The issue of advertising to children was one of the most important covered in the hearings. The weight of the testimony and supporting data on this topic far outstripped any other. However, as our review ... has indicated, there is a great deal of conflict in viewpoint, and little hard data which can be used in resolving it ... Lack of understanding as to how television advertising affects the child has been a major impediment to better regulation of children's television. A great deal remains to be known, especially with regard to second order effects such as ramifications for consumer socialization and family relationships". Pierre Juneau, Chair of the Canadian Radio Television and Telecommunication Commission commented in 1973 that " ... These hearings have proved that we still require much proof before the long range effect of television advertising to children on the child's development and on family interaction can be established ... The commission is hard pressed to make general recommendations based on a sense of outrage ... it is unable, on its own, to take a sweeping stand as if this was a black and white moral issue. House of Commons, Canada *Standing Committee on Broadcasting, Films and Assistance to the Arts* July 5, 1973.

measure questions such as the age at which children understood the
nature of advertising, and the impact of advertising on children's choices
and on parent-child relationships. Much of this research was conducted
by academics from psychology or business faculties and was positivistic
in orientation, often using experimental designs. The assumption that
more hard data would lead to clear policy choices did not transpire
and at least in the USA the research produced greater complexity than
clarity.[14] The most extensive use of social science evidence in policy
making occurred in the famous Federal Trade Commission rulemaking
proceedings of the late 1970s. The facts established were that advertising
does persuade children to ask for advertised products, that these requests
sometimes cause mild conflicts between parent and child and that
parents yielded to the requests. The Final Staff report of the Commission
rulemaking concluded that children from two to six are unable to fully
understand child-oriented advertising:

"They place indiscriminate trust in the selling message. They do not correctly
perceive persuasive bias in advertising, and their life experience is insufficient
to help them counter argue. Finally, the content, placement and various
techniques used in child-oriented television commercials attract children and
enhance the advertising and the product. As a result, children are not able
to evaluate adequately child-oriented advertising."

A comprehensive review of the social science literature by Young in
1990 concluded that there remains significant uncertainty in the literature over such issues as when children develop the ability to understand
and counter argue against the effects of advertising. There seems to be
a consensus that understanding makes a significant change in middle
childhood around seven or eight but the ability to identify "persuasive
intent" seems to develop sometime between this age and 10 or 11.
There is some evidence that advertising sharpens sex role stereotyping,
influences the type of food products that children ask for and causes
conflicts between parents and children. He also noted that much of the
research has concentrated on short term impact and specific advertising
practices[15] There has been little attempt to measure the long term

---

[14] Weiss argues that "[as] more studies are done, they often elaborate rather than simplify.
They generate complex, varied and even contradictory views of the social phenomena
under study. C. Weiss, "The Many Meanings of Research Utilization" in M. Blumler,
ed., *Social Science and Social Policy* (1986) p. 39.
[15] See B. Young *Television Advertising and Children* (1990), p. 40.

cultural effects even though this is often a basic concern of critics of children's advertising.

He concludes that the literature indicates many contradictory findings, some methodological problems and a general lack of theoretical development. These are perhaps standard academic critiques of policy-driven work. However, he also suggests that the research was often grounded in specific cultural assumptions about television advertising being a threat that children may find difficult to resist. The cultural assumption of the child as innocent, which reflects particular historical and ethnocentric view of childhood, was embedded within many studies. Although some studies[16] surveyed challenged these assumptions most made no attempt to problematise this common sense assumption. There was also within several studies the image of the child as an embryonic adult developing through stages to a full-blown rationality, hence the emphasis on the stage at which children understand "selling intent" and are able to argue against advertising's persuasion. This approach may overemphasise the distinction between the ability of adults and children to "argue against" advertising, positing a sharp contrast between adult rationality and childlike credulousness.

More recent work, influenced by cultural studies, has suggested that children are much more active agents in decoding television messages and that this process takes place in the context of family and peer culture. Hodge and Tripp, drawing on interpretive rather than empirical approaches, attempt to understand how children make sense of their world and through interaction with the social world construct their subjectivity. They argue that children may develop subversive meanings from television texts and images, and that children interpret programmes within their own social milieu. They question the conception of children as "imperfectly socialized miniature adults" with its implicit downplaying of children's culture and argue that children are able to handle significant complexity of meaning in television programming.[17]

---

[16] See, e.g. J. Esserman, *Television Advertising and Children: Issues, Research and Findings* (1981) and L. Donohue, L. Henke and W. Donohue, "Do Kids know what TV commercials intend?" (1980) 20:5 *Journal of Advertising Research* 51 which claimed that earlier research in the 1970s had underestimated the abilities of children to understand commercials. Young critiques both these studies at pp. 83–94 and is particularly critical of the Donohue study. Both Esserman and Donohue acted as industry experts in Federal hearings and Esserman advised the lawyers acting for the toy company in the *Irwin Toy* litigation.

[17] See "Conclusion" in B. Hodge and D. Tripp *Children and Television* (1986), Chap. 8.

They do not view their research as a defence of current television programming but argue that there is a need to understand the inter-action of television messages with issues of class, gender, race and family dynamics. Seiter argues that commercial advertising and children's programming capitalises on a long tradition of subversive values in childrens' literature which rejects parental authority and pokes fun at adult institutions.[18] These more recent developments call into question assumptions about the child as innocent and advertising as seduction and question any simple denunciation of children's programming.

There does not appear to be currently a clear empirical basis for more rational and effective policymaking. Hodge and Tripp argue that the obsessive concerns with objective proof of the effects of television on children may be misguided.[19] Given these uncertainties it is therefore interesting to understand how "law's truth" has conceptualised the power of advertising over children.

In the 1970s The Federal Trade Commission Staff Report had argued that television advertising to children who were unable to understand the selling purpose of advertising was unfair and deceptive. This reflected the imbalance in power between large advertisers and individuals who were "psychologically, intellectually and economically" at the opposite pole from "the traditionally assumed 'rational consumer' for whom advertising provides a service".[20] Traditional common law doctrines in relation to contract and tort, such as the contractual incapacity of minors and the "attractive nuisance"[21] doctrine, which protected children from their lack of judgment, supported this position. The Report had also argued that advertising of highly sugared products to any children was unfair and deceptive because of the potential injury to children's health, the naivety of the children's audience and the manipulative nature of the advertising. The Report viewed this general argument as supported by its developing jurisprudence on section 5 of the Federal Trade Commission Act which declares to be unlawful "unfair methods of competition in or affecting commerce, and unfair or deceptive acts or practices in or affecting commerce".[22] The idea of

---

[18] See E. Seiter, *Sold Separately: Parents and Children in Consumer Culture* (1995), p. 232.

[19] See B. Hodge and D. Tripp, *Children and Television* (1986), p. 2.

[20] *Federal Trade Commission Staff Report op. cit.*, pp. 28–29.

[21] The "attractive nuisance" doctrine requires adults who maintain attractive but danger-ous premises to take special care to make them "child-proof".

[22] The Commission cited to cases such as the argument for the prohibition of vitamin advertising to children (*Hudson Pharmaceutical Corp.* 89 F.T.C. 82 (1977)) and the finding

unfairness at this time reflected a three prong test, (1) whether the practice offends public policy "within at least the penumbra of some common law, statutory, or other established concept of unfairness" (2) whether it is immoral, unethical or unscrupulous and (3) whether it causes substantial injury to consumers or competitors or both.[23] The flavour of the Staff Report is found in their finding that television advertising to children was unethical:

> "The relationship between the present advertisers and the child audience is 'unconscionable' ... sophisticated, well-financed adults are advertising potentially harmful products, via the most powerful medium ever devised for reaching young children, to an audience which has little understanding either of the means by which it is being manipulated or of the potential harms in the products. The advantage in this encounter of extremes lies overwhelmingly—if not indeed, wholly—with the powerful side."[24]

As I indicated above, the attempts by the Commission to regulate advertising to children were thwarted by business interests and the Final Report of the Commission in 1981 which terminated the rule-making, was a capitulation. It drew very narrow conclusions on research findings in relation to advertising to children since it feared that any potentially arguable conclusion would expose the Commission to further attack by business. The findings and approach of the Commission resurfaced however in Canada in the decision of the Canadian Supreme Court in *Irwin Toy Ltd. v. Attorney General of Quebec*.[25] This case arose out of a challenge by Irwin Toy, a major Canadian toy manufacturer, to Quebec legislation which prohibits advertising directed at children under 13 years. The legislation was challenged as a contravention of the freedom of expression provisions in the Canadian Charter of Rights and Freedoms. The court confirmed in *Irwin Toy* that advertising, as

---

that a fantasy growth sequence in advertising for Wonderbread misleadingly implied that Wonderbread had magical growth inducing properites (*ITT Continental Baking* 83 F.T.C. 865 (1973)).
[23] This was based on approval of the approach taken in the "Cigarette Rule", *Unfair or Deceptive Advertising and Labelling of Cigarettes in Relation to the Health Hazards of Smoking, Statement of Basis and Purpose* 29 Fed. Reg. 8324 (1964) approved in *F.T.C. v. Sperry and Hutchinson Co.* 405 U.S. 233, 244 (1972). But see now market model of unfairness reproduced as Appendix to *Re International Harvester Co.* 104 F.T.C. 949, 1070 (1985).
[24] See E. Ratner, J. Hellegers, G. Stern *et al. Federal Trade Commission Staff Report on Television Advertising to Children* (1978), p. 220.
[25] [1989] 1 S.C.R. 927.

commercial speech, was protected under the freedom of expression provision of the Charter. However, legislation may be saved under section 1 of the Charter if the government proves that the limitations on the right are demonstrably justifiable as reasonable restrictions in a free and democratic society. The court had developed a test, similar to one developed earlier by the U.S. Supreme Court,[26] for determining this question. Under section 1, the government is required to show that the objective of the law relates to a pressing and substantial objective and that the means chosen to achieve that objective are proportional to the objectives. This requires that the measures chosen are rationally connected to the objective, minimally impair the guaranteed right and the deleterious effects of the law do not outweigh the beneficial effects of the law.

The judgment of the majority, delivered by Dickson C.J., upheld the legislation, primarily on a manipulation thesis. The term "manipulation" is used repeatedly in the judgment; the concern identified by the legislature is that of "the protection of a group which is particularly vulnerable to the techniques of seduction and manipulation abundant in advertising" and "accords with a general goal of consumer protection legislation, viz; to protect a group that is most vulnerable to commercial manipulation".[27] The judgment establishes a legal common sense that children are innocents and advertising is seduction. He identifies several particular concerns: "the particular susceptibility of young children to media manipulation, their inability to differentiate between reality and fiction and to grasp the persuasive intention behind the message, and the secondary effects of exterior influences on the family and parental authority".[28] In order to establish a factual basis for this concern the court relied on the conclusions of the Federal Trade Commission in relation to television advertising to children under seven years old. This report confirmed Dickson C.J.'s judgment that "advertising directed at young children is *per se* manipulative ... [and] aims to promote products by convincing those who will always believe."[29]

Science seemed, therefore to buttress law's common sense. But

[26] See *Central Hudson Gas & Electric Corp. v. Public Service Commission of New York* 447 U.S. 557 (1980).
[27] *Irwin Toy op. cit.*, Dickson C.J. at 990.
[28] *ibid.*, at 987.
[29] *ibid.*, at 988.

science did not in fact answer the question before the court since the F.T.C. conclusions related only to television advertising and to children under seven, whereas the Quebec legislation related to all forms of advertising and included children under 13. Moreover, there is surely something rather abstract about the harm caused to children under six by their inability to understand commercials. It is rare for children under six to make economic purchasing decisions, so that their purchase requests will be filtered through their parents. Perhaps this should have led the court to focus on the damage done to family relationships by children demanding products which they had seen on television, but the court declined this invitation perhaps because the Final Report of the Commission failed to reach any conclusion on family conflicts caused by children nagging parents for products advertised on television.

The majority judgment extended the conclusions of the F.T.C. in two ways. First, it thought that it was reasonable to conclude that the conclusion could be extended to advertising in other media and to advertising aimed at older children (7–12). The court cites no specific social science evidence to support these extensions. In truth the issue of when children are able to "argue against" advertising remains controversial. The attorneys for the Quebec Office of Consumer Protection had cited a study to the court which seemed to support the argument that although children understood the nature of advertisements it was not until 11 or 12 that they could convincingly argue against the messages.[30] But there certainly was no consensus in the scientific literature. Perhaps sensing this lack of empirical support, the majority also argued that the court should show deference to a legislative decision in the area of balancing competing economic and social interests where there was incomplete scientific evidence. In addition, since the ban could be rationalised as only partial—advertisers were still able to direct advertising to adults, the means chosen was not disproportionate to the objective to be achieved.

In fact, social science evidence had played little role in the introduction of the Quebec legislation. During legislative debates on an early version of the Bill, the relevant minister responded to arguments

---

[30] See D. Roedder, B. Sternthal and B. Calder, "Attitude-Behavior Consistency in children's response to television advertising" (1983) 20 *Journal of Marketing Research* 337.

for more studies by stating that "we wish that more studies will be conducted ... we ought however to take our responsibilities now and not wait for the results of studies which may be contradicted by other later studies". There was an opinion poll at the time which showed strong support for a ban and this seemed of greater importance than empirical data.

The majority judgment in *Irwin Toy* reproduces the rationality/ manipulation dichotomy in the legal analysis of advertising. Regulation is justifiable to protect the vulnerable, such as children, who are not able to protect themselves against advertising and who cannot tell fact from fantasy. The legal subject is either coherent rational and freely choosing or subject to some form of disability which impairs their judgment and necessitates the paternalistic protection of the state. We encounter a similar dichotomy to the reasonable/credulous distinction in the law of misleading advertising. But the dissenting judgment of McIntyre J., noting that "there was evidence that children are incapable of distinguishing fact from fiction in advertising" comments that "this is hardly surprising: many adults have the same problem".[31] McIntyre J. does not tease out this insight to make the more general argument that advertising is often about fantasy and symbols, that adults "buy in" to symbols associated with commodities. The law hesitates to conclude that this type of behaviour indicates manipulation rather than rational behaviour. An acceptance of such a conclusion would lead to the proscription of much lifestyle advertising, which many adult consumers seem to have difficulty in "arguing against".

Advertising to children raises broader questions about the conceptualisation of advertising in legal discourse. These broader questions are exposed by an examination of the politics of children's advertising. Unlike many consumer issues it cannot be understood in purely economic terms or issues of redistribution of economic resources. In both Canada and the U.S. the debate was often drawn in terms of the boundaries of the market and the family, the public and the private. Childhood was regarded as a separate sphere of paramount importance to personal development. The intrusion of the commercial marketplace with its low quality programmes and commercial values hindered children's development, engendered family conflict and undermined parental authority. In Quebec, and the rest of Canada, concerns over

---

[31] McIntyre J. at 1007.

advertising to children were also intertwined with concerns about the Americanisation of Canadian life. The rise of opposition to advertising to children may be viewed as a partial response to the increasing colonisation of the family by commodity relations, with capitalistic values extending beyond work relations to those traditionally included within the private realm, including the worlds of leisure and the family.[32] The movement around children's advertising was animated by values rather than interests and was successful in transforming a private family issue into a major public and political issue.

The response of advertisers to the concerns was essentially ". . . prove the harm from advertising" . . . and "the content of children's viewing is a private matter for parents to determine". Banning of advertising to children, in their view, not only raised issues of free speech but was an unwarranted interference in the private sphere of family choice substituting the governmental nanny for parental authority.

Critiques of advertising to children often seem to be a combination of specific arguments of harm, which are difficult to prove, combined with more general critiques of the inculcation in children of the materialistic values of consumer capitalism. Children are innocents seduced by the shallow values of cartoons, and the mindless programming of children's television. "Big business need their youngsters compliant, vulnerable and hooked on their fads, fashions and addictions".[33]

The analyses of cultural studies suggest the value of analysis of children's advertising through the prisms of class, gender and race. Seiter raises the question whether much of the criticism of advertising to children is simply middle-class disdain for popular culture. She indicates that currently many middle-class parents in the USA believe that they can shield their children from commercials through the purchase of videos and the use of cable television. Yet ironically she points out that there is often much subtle commercialism on these quality channels and the supposed quality children's stories are often violent and contain as many stereotypes as cartoon culture. The children's story of *Babar the Elephant* is described by one non-commercial channel as a "children's classic with time honoured morals". Not only is this programme tied in to the sale of stuffed animals in middle-class

---

[32] This was the thesis of Larose in relation to the movement to abolish advertising to children in Quebec. See G. Larose, above n. 90.

[33] R. Nader, quoted in R. Collins, above, n. 10.

toy stores but Ariel Dorfman has shown how Babar can be viewed as a deeply racist and imperialist story.[34]

Seiter's arguments are influenced by Bourdieu's theory of cultural capital and its connection to class domination. This may be one way of understanding the rulemaking proceedings before the Federal Trade Commission in the late 70s, when many individuals from the professional classes, doctors, teachers and so on, provided testimony to the Commission about their fears over consumer culture. These hearings run to thousands of pages of testimony and were focused ostensibly on establishing whether there was a reliable basis of evidence for concluding that advertising harmed children. Yet the hearing transcripts often read like a conflict between holders of cultural capital (represented by middle-class professionals, university professors and others) and pure money capital represented by the media and business. It is possible that these holders of cultural capital were appalled at the developing dispositions of their children to prefer Ronald McDonald and Barbie as cultural icons rather than middle-class norms. For example, the following extract is from the testimony of Robert Abramovitz, a child psychiatrist and Associate Professor of Paediatrics at Yale University Child Study Center:

> "I feel harm results in ... instilling imperious acquisitive values and habits which include desires for habits, and which promote indulgence of all wants and interfere with the development of the ability to delay gratification.
>
> ... I am certainly greatly concerned that if you get a young child starting at age $2\frac{1}{2}$, and you begin to tell them that their self-worth depends on acquiring products, and you pile up those associations over many years, that has a strong contributing part to play in their later on having the belief that their self-worth is directly related to materialism and consumerism.
>
> I think we have to face the fact that materialism and consumerism are not necessarily considered serious personality problems in this country, but I think that they ought to be looked at that way".[35]

Similar comments were made by other experts. Concerns over advertising to children seem to represent some strands of the mass culture debates of the 1950s where there was middle-class concern over the

---

[34] Seiter, *op. cit.*, p. 110. A. Dorfman, *The Emperor's Old Clothes: What the Lone Ranger, Babar, the Reader's Digest, and other False Friends do to Our Minds* (1983).
[35] In the Matter of Children's Advertising Transcript of Hearings at 6336 and 6345.

corrosive effects of popular culture, particularly on young people.[36] These debates represent a conflict between holders of cultural capital and economic capital (the broadcasters, advertisers and industry).

The battles over children's advertising in the USA might be viewed as surrogates for more general class conflicts over who establishes the ground rules of consumer capitalism, and the impact of this culture on social life. It is a conflict over the power of corporate culture and its values. Lynn Spigel argues that:

"The child ... becomes an alibi and a conduit for larger issues regarding the commercialization of communication ... the discourse of victimization that surrounds the child viewer might ... usefully be renamed and rein-vestigated as a discourse of power through which adults express their own disenfranchisement from our nation's dominant mode of communication".[37]

Tom Englehart, in a perceptive essay on advertising to children in the 1980s, hypothesised that the periodic concerns about advertising to children were metaphors for adults' reflections on the type of society we had become:

"Ideally we want to think of them as belonging to another race of beings, rather like the little denizens of Strawberry land, innocents open to the best we can possibly teach. We want to see them as different, more sensitive, somehow more human than ourselves, and so children's TV offends in ways the usual critiques do not touch. It disturbs because we shudder to see our children attracted to balder versions of what we are attracted to. Perhaps many of us also want to see ourselves as more immune to consumer dreams ... than we are, so that it's like meeting yourself naked on a busy street in some hideously embarrassing dream to see your child ... hunker down to watch a morning of kid vid. But why, after all, should the kids who live in our houses *not* be attracted to what, in slightly more sophisticated form, is meant to attract us all: dreams of buying glitzy toys (promising more than they can ever deliver) with which to play out our fantasies".[38]

It is clear who has currently won this class debate. The growth of

[36] See discussion and further reference to the "mass culture" debates in C. Mukerji and M. Schudson eds., *Rethinking Popular Culture: Contemporary Perspectives in Cultural Studies* (1991), p. 27.
[37] L. Spigel, "Seducing the Innocents" in *Ruthless Criticism: New Perspectives in U.S. Communications History* (R.W. McChesney ed. 1993) at 283.
[38] T. Englehart, *op. cit.*, p. 110.

designer clothes for children and the permeation of fashion and style
to infants as represented by Baby Gap stores, suggests that critics of
advertising to children have had little impact in stemming the tide of
commercialism in the media and children's culture. The Children's
Television Act of 1990 in the United States merely restores the status
quo before the deregulation of the 1980s. There are important lessons
from these attempts to regulate advertising to children. The U.S.
experience indicates that the power of business and broadcasting
interests can be formidable in relation to any proposal which appears to
threaten advertising. The alliance of the culture industries of consumer
capitalism and the First Amendment, probably one of the few widely
known constitutional amendments, make a powerful adversary. Ralph
Nader prophetically warned Michael Pertschuk, then Chair of the
Federal Trade Commission, at the inception of the children's advertising
rulemaking that "[i]f you take on the advertisers you'll end up with
so many regulators—with their bones bleached—in the desert".[39]

Attention to issues of class, gender and race might permit analysis
to go beyond the existing structures of argument around advertising to
children. The defence of advertisers is that if one cannot prove harm
through behavioural data, then the critics of advertising to children are
elitists and anti-democratic, wishing to substitute their preferences,
through the state, for those of the ordinary viewer. Advertisers wish to
preserve the private world of the family from the public intervention
of the state. The arguments are similar to those made in relation to
commercial speech and market regulation. Parental choice in relation
to advertising to children substitutes for individual choices in the
market. At the same time critics of advertising to children have
sometimes constructed the family as a haven from the heartless world
of commercialism. There is within both these characterisations the
illusion that "the family is a private place, a haven of protected positive
emotions safe from the stresses of public labour, commercialism and
power."[40]

---

[39] Quoted in "Mike Pertschuk and the Federal Trade Commission" case prepared by A.
Applbaum under the supervision of Stephanie Gould, John F. Kennedy School of
Government, Harvard University, p. 15.

[40] A. Oakley, "Normal Motherhood: An Exercise in Self-Control?" in *Controlling Women:
The Normal and the Deviant* (B. Hutter and G. Williams eds., 1981), quoted in S. Gavigan,
"Women and Abortion in Canada: What's Law Got to Do with It?" in *Feminism and
Political Economy: Women's Work, Women's Struggles*" (H. Maroney and M. Luxton eds.
1987), p. 269.

It might be useful to note the role of television and advertising within the household economy of differing classes. Management of the household economy remains women's sphere, and working-class parents or single parents may have greater pressure on their time and less resources to spend on alternatives to television as a form of baby-sitter. The consumer society has not in fact reduced but increased many women's unpaid labour in the home.[41] Working-class women are unlikely to have as easy access to the educational and high quality videos of middle-class parents. Their choices in this market are constrained. At the same time it is quite possible that popular culture on commercial television, and associated toys such as "My Little Pony", are frowned upon at their children's schools and experts make them feel guilty about allowing their children to passively watch television. They are, therefore, to blame if their children do not seem to progress as fast educationally as middle-class children. For legislators and policy-makers (still generally male-dominated) to state glibly that advertising to children is a private matter for parents obscures the politics of gender and class of the household economy.

Moreover it is difficult to view media watching as a purely "private choice" of parents. The media is so deeply part of public culture that any children cut off from this culture would have difficulties relating to their peers. One of the characteristics of consumer culture is the mingling of the private and the public world. But there is little democratic control over this culture in a commercially dominated system.

Advertising to children also illuminates the limitations of existing legal and public policy discourse with the dichotomy of the rational adult and the manipulated child. It understates the continuities between advertising to both groups, and overdraws the extent to which adults make coolly rational purchasing decisions.

The above comments are not intended to suggest some complacent quietism about advertising to children. The ubiquity of television in society provides access to consumer culture for many who are unable to afford the trappings of consumer culture. Black writers in the USA argue that this has a devastating effect on poor black children who are unable to buy the status symbols of consumption and that this frustration

---

[41] See Seiter *op. cit.*, at p. 18 and see D. Hayden, *Redesigning the American Dream: The Future of Housing, Work and Family Life* (1984).

leads to conflict and aggression.[42] In addition, Seiter notes that children's commercials often "reproduce race and gender hierarchies while they speak to democratic, utopian themes".[43] The growth of commercial advertising to children in Europe may exacerbate class distinctions between those who are able to afford high-quality alternatives for their children and the accompanying "educational" toys, and other parents.

The issues raised by children's advertising may therefore not be dissimilar from cultural questions about advertising and the dominance of commercial values. The myth of childhood as a separate sphere filled with innocents is primarily a Northern European creation of the nineteenth-century middle-class. There is a danger that we accept this myth and blame television advertising for inappropriate behaviour and for polluting the innocence of childhood. There is the further danger of nostalgia for some pre-electronic media age when families were families, children were sweetness and light ... and women knew their place. That is undoubtedly not what animates many critics of advertising to children but for progressives concerned about consumer culture it is important not to confuse serious critique of commercialism of children's culture with simple moralisms.

4 Cultural Domination, Equality and Unfair Cultural Practices

INTRODUCTION: THE ROUTINE AND THE SPECTACULAR

The university at which I teach has a student body, significant numbers of which are drawn from a broad cross-section of the multicultural community of Toronto. The university prides itself on this fact when compared to the older, traditionally more WASP dominated, University of Toronto. I was in the University bookstore one day and noticed that there was a large mock-up of a new student centre which was to be built shortly. There was also an artist's rendition of the mall, complete

---

[42] See R. Austin, "A Nation of Thieves: Securing Black Peoples Right to Shop and Sell in White America" (1994) *Utah L. Rev. 147* citing Carl Nightingale, *On the Edge: A History of Poor Black Children and Their American Dreams* (1993), pp. 125–126.
[43] Seiter *op. cit.*, p. 143.

with students milling in the mall. I noticed that all the students in the picture were white. This jarred with the image of the University. On returning to my office I phoned the head of the bookstore to point out this fact and that it seemed inappropriate to have this painting in a multicultural university. I believe that he assumed that I was slightly wacky and by the end of the conversation he had equated me with book burners and censors. I then wrote a letter to the representative of the development company on the campus. I received a reply that essentially stated that it was "merely an artist's mock up" with the implication that I was overreacting. By this time I was becoming more and more outraged but also less sure of my position. My partner supported me but I was not confident to speak widely about the incident. I had, fortunately, copied my letter to the University president. When I passed by the bookstore a couple of days later the display had disappeared. On returning to my office there was a cryptic note from the President indicating that he had heard that I had been given "the run around" and shortly after a senior official from the development company phoned to apologise for the mistake.

There was nothing outrageous about the artist's rendition. Challenging the common sense that "it's just a picture", that its innocuous, that no one would really notice it as part of the routine of everyday life and so on is not straightforward. But studies of advertising images suggest that we are repeatedly invited to buy into primary and secondary meanings in advertisements as part of the routine of everyday life. They become part of common sense.

These cultural representations may reinforce cultural oppression, economic dominance and economic exclusion of people constructed as different or inferior. Racism and sexism may be secreted in the interstices of everyday life and common sense. They are cultural constructions which are not to be equated simply with overt acts of racism. Racist stereotypes have a long history in Europe and North America. Some of these include black women as either matriarchs or dangerously seductive, black men as either "good", upwardly mobile individuals conforming to U.S. middle-class norms or "bad" blacks, irresponsible members of the underclass, inhabiting the ghetto.

"Good blacks are displayed in advertising, sit-coms and public forums, whereas Bad blacks ... are featured on the cop shows, rap videos and news programmes, with "badness" serving as a badge of honour or sign of disapproval, depending where one stands in relation to the system. These two sets of images interact, in that Good Blacks are portrayed as spokespersons for the bad, while the apparent success of one category defeats the special treatment (positive or affirmative action) on the part of the other".[44]

bell hooks describes how many advertisements "depict a white heterosexual couple engaged in some "fun" activity while a lone black, male friend looks on with longing and envy". She sees this as part of a re-presentation of the idea that blacks should seek to succeed within the white-dominated system and in terms of its values. Black men work "hard to be rewarded by the great white father within the existing system."[45] In a different context Bordo makes a similar argument against the idea of "fashion as resistance". She argues that there are deeply sedimented cultural beliefs about the women's bodies and that it was difficult to challenge them.

Advertising is also part of the media system and Van Dijk in his study of elite discourse and racism indicated the convergence of many factors in racism in the media.[46] He noted the difficulties which minorities face in being hired in the media: the extent to which the coverage of ethnic affairs revolved around issues of immigration, crime, drugs, violence and rioting: cultural differences are negatively interpreted as the cause of many social problems: discrimination is dealt with as discrete incidents: white elites are quoted more extensively and credibly than representatives of minority groups: whites and British institutions are presented as tolerant and ethnic groups are implicitly presented as a problem if not a threat.[47]

Advertising stereotypes must be seen against this background and in this section I explore whether law is likely to be a significant challenge to racist and sexist stereotyping and the extent to which the law might develop theories of advertising as an unfair cultural practice.[48] Legal regulation of advertising has focused traditionally on issues of misleading advertising, based on either the concept of truth or information. The harm from misleading advertising in terms of consumer and competitor losses could be readily identified. There has not been however a clear

---

[44] J.N. Pietersee, *White on Black: Images of Africa and Blacks in Western Popular Culture* (1992), p. 203.
[45] b. hooks, "Doing it for Daddy" in *Constructing Masculinity* M. Berger, B. Wallis, and S. Watson eds. (1995), p. 101.
[46] See T. Van Dijk, *Elite Discourse and Racism* (1993) Chap. 7 "Media Discourse".
[47] *ibid.*, pp. 244–282.
[48] See K. Sullivan, *op. cit.*, Chap. 1, n. 8.

theory for regulation of exploitative and unfair advertising and there remains significant disagreement concerning the harm from these forms of advertising.

At one time concerns about sexism and racism in advertising in consumer markets were often conceptualised as questions of "taste and decency". Sexist advertising was offensive because it offended taste and decency. Since taste and decency were viewed as subjective, however, questions about racist and sexist representations were often allotted to self-regulatory rather than legal procedures. They were constructed as issues on which, as with other issues of taste, reasonable people might agree to differ.

One of the important transformations of recent decades is to view these issues now through the lens of equality, dignity and autonomy. The images are no longer innocent questions of private taste but implicate important public values. Feminism and cultural studies underlined the importance of everyday images in sustaining oppression. Writers on consumer law have been slow to notice this insight or the fact that discrimination in consumption markets may be fuelled by cultural stereotypes which may in turn be fuelled by advertising stereotypes.

There are a number of existing aspects of laws and "soft law" which might provide the basis for regulation of advertising images in this area. There exists in many countries, regulation of unfair trade practices. In several European countries these statutes refer to "honest practices", implicating ethical norms of trading. Section 1 of the German Law Against Unfair Competition includes the broad prohibition of acts that are contrary to "honest practices". This legislation has been interpreted to include demeaning portrayals of individuals or groups.[49] The Federal Trade Commission has historically interpreted its mandate in relation to "unfair acts or practices" to include those that are "immoral, unethical or unscrupulous". This mandate could require a decision maker to apply conceptions of community standards and the measures in this paragraph might be described as the community standards approach.

A second approach is to view the issue in terms of human rights to

---

[49] See below, p. 126 and see S. Sverdrup and E. Sto, "Regulation of Sex Discrimination in Advertising: An Empirical Inquiry into the Norwegian Case" (1992) 14 *Journal of Consumer Policy* 371: A. Peltonen, "Preliminary Ruling on Discriminatory Advertising" (1995) 18 *Journal of Consumer Policy* 219.

dignity and equality. In many countries there are prohibitions on discrimination in the provision of goods and services and article 3 of the International Code of Advertising Practice sponsored by the International Chamber of Commerce states that "advertisements should avoid endorsing discrimination based upon race, religion or sex." One strand of feminist analysis has emphasised the harmful images of women in advertising, the barriers which such images may create for the achievement of equality, and connections between demeaning images and violence against women. This argument has been recognised by the Supreme Court of Canada in relation to pornographic images[50] which use similar techniques to advertising. Minority groups in the USA have also argued that there should be legal recognition of the damage done to minorities by racist speech. There should be greater acknowledgement of the fact that "words and images wound"[51] and that these images may be part of a larger cultural domination which should be recognised in human rights adjudication, for example, by incorporating the victim's perspective rather than merely looking at how a reasonable person or average reader would interpret images or acts.[52] Advertising regulation to foster equality goals has engendered controversy since it appears to restrict freedom of speech. This issue is raised most starkly in the U.S. where free speech is an important ideology. This apparent conflict prompted Catherine MacKinnon to claim that in the regulation of images, the "law of equality and the law of freedom of speech are on a collision course".[53]

There are, therefore, a number of legal sources for the development of theories of advertising regulation which recognise that advertising may be an unfair cultural practice.[54] This is also an area where "soft law", such as codes of practice and guidelines, are prominent. The rationales for soft law are that it may be difficult to frame clear standards for the regulation of images, and that soft law may be more

---

[50] See below R. v. Butler.
[51] See R. Delgado, "Words that Wound: A Tort Action for Racial Insults, Epithets and Name Calling" (1982) 17 Harvard Civil Rights and Civil liberties Law Review 133.
[52] See discussion in M. Chamallas, "Structuralist and Cultural Domination Theories meet Title VII: Some Contemporary Influences" (1994) 92 Mich L. Rev. 2370 where the author includes under cultural domination theories such writers as Derrick Bell author of And We are Not Saved: The Elusive Quest for Racial Justice (1987) and Mari Matsuda et. al. Words that Wound: Critical Race Theory, Assaultive Speech and The First Amendment (1993).
[53] C. MacKinnon Only Words (1993), p. 71.
[54] K. Sullivan, op. cit.

flexible on "sensitive" issues such as taste and decency. If the question of sexism and racism in the media and advertising is conceptualised as a question of human rights then there may be less justification for referring these issues to soft law norms.

(1) Soft law: Unfair Advertising and the Advertising Standards Authority in the U.K.

The U.K. Code of Advertising Practice contains a clause which indicates that "advertisements should contain nothing that is likely to cause serious or widespread offence. Particular care should be taken to avoid causing offence on the grounds of race, religion, sex, sexual orientation or disability". Each advertisement is assessed in the context of the particular advertisement and "the standards of decency and propriety that are generally accepted in the UK".[55] The Authority has the power under the code to ask the media not to carry the advertisement, thereby barring the publication of the offending advertisement. In addition, adverse publicity may accrue to the advertiser, since the Authority publishes monthly reports and cases are often reported in the general media. A celebrated recent case is that of advertisements by Benetton, the clothing manufacturer, which included pictures of a naked new-born baby and which produced more complaints than the ASA had ever received about a single advertisement. Other controversial advertisements included a picture of a man dying of AIDS, a nun kissing a priest, and an advertisement that couples an angelic white child with a black child who appears to have horns.

The underlying theory of regulation adopted by the ASA is that the advertisement will have contraved the code if it causes "serious or widespread offence". In a seminar sponsored by the ASA on this topic, involving various representatives of interest groups, this phrase was widely believed to reflect the "need for good manners". They also recognised the need "for sensitivity" in the portrayal of ethnic minorities since "minorities may be more sensitive" and advertising standards cannot "simply be seen in terms of what majorities find acceptable."[56]

The system of self-regulation is primarily complaint based and apparently the majority of complainants tend to be from older, middle-

---

[55] See *The British Codes of Advertising and Sales Promotion*, rule 5.1 and *Advertising Standards Authority Monthly Report 22*, March 1993.
[56] See *Monthly Report 22* (1993).

class, and better educated consumers.[57] Analysis of the advertisements
by the staff of the ASA under the taste and decency clause is based
primarily on an investigation of the context, medium, product, and
audience against the background of prevailing standards of decency.
The Authority appears to react most strongly to obviously aggressive
forms of advertising portrayal as represented by Benetton or an
advertisement for Linn Hi-Fi which showed a picture of a young
woman with the caption "She's terrific in bed. She's witty, intelligent
and makes her own pasta. She doesn't have a Linn Hi-Fi. But her
sister does, and she's the one I married."

    It is instructive to analyse some examples of the jurisprudence under
this section drawn randomly from the Monthly Reports of complaint
activity. One advertisement in the magazine *Mixmag* featured a naked
woman bending over and covering her genitalia with her hand and
the trap-line "open all hours". The Authority upheld the complaint,
considering the advertisement to be "extremely offensive". A second
advertisement for cattlefeed mixture in the *British Dairying Magazine*
featured a young woman in jeans and a T-shirt, in a very deserted
field, below the headline "A VERY TASTY PROPOSITION". This
complaint was not upheld primarily because it "was unlikely to cause
widespread offence to readers of the magazine". A third advertisement
was a poster for a radio station which catered to 15–35 years olds,
which showed a close up of "part of a woman" who was standing with
her legs apart and wearing brief denim shorts, above the headline
"Jammin". The authority did not uphold the complaint since it considered that the image was unlikely to cause widespread offence. Finally,
a poster for a computer game headed "BEAT THE TRAFFIC"
included the slogan "ITS A RACE RIOT". The poster showed various
caricatures including, in the foreground, a snarling black man dressed
as a tribal warrior. The authority upheld the complaint but considered
that "the presentation of the characters was unlikely to cause serious
offence but found the slogan to be insensitive and was therefore pleased
to note that it would be withdrawn".

    These examples seem to suggest[58] that the obvious and outrageous
will be sanctioned but that the authority does not address the subtleties
of advertising techniques such as the use of blocking (showing individuals

---

[57] Interview, Philip Rubinstein, Advertising Standards Authority, June 21, 1994.
[58] My conclusions here are tentative and based on the ASA case reports. I have not
    studied the actual advertisements and this limits any more profound analysis.

merely as body parts) as in the case of the focus on a woman's crotch in the advertisement for jeans. The authority focuses on the "insensitivity" of the portrayal of blacks, rather than the fact that the illustration seemed to invite consumers to see and reproduce traditional stereotypes of black people in English colonial history as primitive savages, thereby contravening values of equality and dignity.

The many complaints concerning Benetton's advertisements deserve further comment. The outrage represented by these complaints indicates clearly that in this case many consumers did not immediately "buy in" to the connection between the image and the product. The disjuncture between a patient dying of AIDS and a clothing store selling clothes to young middle-class consumers is too strong. There is no obvious connection between signifier and signified. But why do many people not react to the routine white, emaciated, eurocentric images of female beauty in so many advertisements? Oliviero Toscani, director of advertising for Benetton, attempted to defend their advertising by arguing that it was intended to stimulate debate and draw attention to world problems, pointing out that the images used in the advertisements had all been published previously. A more cynical analysis is that it is a clever technique of marketing to individuals who might regard themselves as young and progressive. They might see the advertisement, and the response to the advertisement, as reflecting middle-class hypocrisies. The company admits that "[c]hallenging authority, attacking prejudices, preaching brotherhood—are tailored to appeal to the younger consumers whom the company covets as consumers".[59] One could even view their ad as a modest form of oppositional discourse to conventional advertising.

I argued in Chapter 3 that I was sceptical of the claim that Benetton advertisements are a serious form of oppositional discourse. My scepticism is not simply that it is about harnessing youthful revolt into commodity purchasing. It is rather that there is, as Bordo argued above (see p. 58) a confusion of resistive pleasure with serious political action. My own impression is that the advertisement did not stimulate debate about the issues in the advertisements but rather about the cleverness of the advertisement and the nature of advertising. Having said that, the Benetton advertisement does pose questions about the criteria to be used in deeming an advertisement to be unfair. Leslie Savan, in a

---

[59] *New York Times News Service,* July 25, 1991.

thoughtful article on Benetton's advertising, concludes that their campaign "makes it that much more difficult for us to sit in unambivalent judgment on what is an exploitative ad."[60] It also illustrates an important institutional issue in the regulation of images and speech. It is possible that bans may have a counter-productive effect by stimulating desire for the controversial idea or image. It is unlikely that Benetton are unaware of this aspect of the controversy surrounding their advertising.

The approach of the ASA and other soft law agencies, which rely on a community standards approach has certain limitations. It follows community standards rather than providing a critical analysis of those standards. It reflects a conventional, rather than a critical, morality of advertising practices. It seems more addressed to questions of offensiveness to readers than to thinking through the harm to groups from the routine repetition of cultural stereotypes. It is unlikely, therefore, to be a major site for challenging these stereotypes.

Canadian soft law includes detailed gender portrayal guidelines which are administered by a self-regulatory organisation. In addition there is a public interest group, MediaWatch, which monitors and criticises the portrayal of women in advertising. It is subsidised by the government and acts as a watchdog. It has good contacts in the media so that it can achieve extensive coverage for any advertising campaign which it criticises. The establishment of a monitoring group has meant that there is a continuing dialogue on the portrayal of women in the media. This may be a potentially valuable form of political activity which does not require the high costs of legal action or loss of control to legal decision-makers.

The potential for using the broad scope of unfair practices legislation to address unfair advertising is exemplified by the recent approach of the German Federal Supreme Court. In 1995 the Court held that certain Benetton advertisements infringed "the general good" under Article 1 of the Federal Unfair Competition Act.[61] The advertisements in question pictured respectively a duck stained by polluted water, small children of the third world at work and part of a human body tattooed "HIV positive". The theory developed by the court was twofold. First, the advertisements concerning pollution and the third world induced

---

[60] L. Savan, *The Sponsored Life* (1994), p. 271.
[61] See [1995] *Wertpapiermitteilungen* 1466, 1470, 1473. My account is based on the English account of the judgment given by Heinrich Doerner in [1995] 3 *Consumer Law Journal* at CS70.

feelings of fear and pity which provoked a desire for solidarity in the consumer, which was then associated with consumption of the products and image of Benetton. This argument is similar to critiques of green advertising which argue that this form of advertising exploits a desire for communal action around the environment by channelling it into being associated with the image and products of the advertiser. Holder notes that a trade magazine provided the tip that green ads should "induce a sense of pride inspired by being part of the movement" and mentions an advertisement for SaaB which stated "sign a petition, lobby your local M.P., form a demonstration, buy a Saab".[62]

The second theory identified by the court in relation to the AIDS advertisement was that it was objectionable because it was an attack on human dignity, in describing AIDS patients as excluded from human society, and inflicted harm on AIDS patients. The court cited in support the comments of an AIDS patient in a French newspaper "during the agony, the sales continue". Within this theory advertising may wreak psychic harm.

These theories of exploitation and exclusion are potentially broad in establishing norms of good practice in advertising.[63] They suggest at the least that there are limits to the intertwining of the public and political with commercialism. This preservation of the public sphere of citizenship from the marketplace contrasts with the citizen as consumer model of the U.S. commercial speech decisions. However the decisions considered in this section tend to set outer limits rather than address potential oppression in the routinised stereotypes in advertising media. They remain critiques of the outrageous periphery rather than the everyday core.

(2) Advertising Images as Exclusion

"Every time I showed them a black face or someone with dark hair or an olive complexion, they would say, 'too dark, Tony' or 'too ethnic'. They wanted to portray the face of British Airways white with a cheesy expression".

(Tony Kaye, advertising executive, quoted in "A world that still washes whiter" *The Independent* February 27, 1996 section 2, p. 14).

---

[62] Jane Holder, "Regulating Green Advertising in the Motor Car Industry" (1991) *Journal of Law and Society* 323 at 330.
[63] For the approach of the Finnish Market Court to Benetton advertising see [1995] *Consumer Law Journal* CS 46.

Exclusion of particular groups in advertising may be a subtle (or not so subtle) method of indicating a racial preference for certain groups. Advertisers choose models so that consumers will identify with the model and the product. As Williamson argues; the advertisement says "hey you" to the identified group, inviting them to see themselves in the advertisement. Advertisements with all-white models may indicate to whites that they are likely to meet individuals of a similar race. Exclusion or absence may subtly dissuade the excluded groups from thinking that this product is for them. These conclusions do not require a great knowledge of advertising techniques. As one U.S. judge commented:

> "It requires no expert to recognize that human models in advertising attempt to create an identification between the model, the consumer, and the product ... [referring to an ad for a housing complex] It is natural that readers of the *Lifestyle* brochure would look at the human models depicted as the kind of individuals that live in and enjoy GSC apartment complexes. If a prospective tenant positively identified with these models, the message conveyed would be that 'I belong in these apartments'. 'My kind of people live there.' Conversely, if the prospective tenant reading the brochure saw no models with whom he or she could identify, the reader would obtain a message that 'these apartments are not for me or my kind'."[64]

The issue of exclusion in advertising has come before the courts in the United States in relation to housing advertisements. There is a long historical record of governmental and non-governmental measures which effectively denied black individuals access to middle-class housing and where there remains clear evidence of continuing discrimination in such areas as mortgage lending practices.[65] The particular issue has been the discriminatory impact of housing advertisements which use all white models in their brochures and advertising. Section 3604 (c) of the Fair Housing Act prohibits the publication of advertisements for real estate which "indicate any preference ... based on race" and in a number of cases advertisers have been sued for repeatedly advertising housing through brochure images with all white models or the virtual

---

[64] *Saunders v. General Services Corporation* 659 F. Supp. 1042 (1986). See the useful discussion of U.S. cases in "Advertising and Title VIII: The Discriminatory Use of Models in Real Estate Advertisements" (1988) 98 *Yale L.J.* 178.
[65] See, *e.g.* G. Squires, *From Redlining to Reinvestment* (1992).

absence of black models. In *Ragin v. New York Times Co.*[66] plaintiffs argued that the *New York Times* had repeatedly violated the Act over a period of 20 years by featuring real estate advertising with virtually no black models. Black models featured only as service employees or in advertisements for housing in predominantly black neighbourhoods. The court rejected the argument that the Act only applied to provocative or offensive advertisements and accepted the argument that the images in the brochures invited consumers to identify with the models in the brochures and that the absence of black models sends the message that blacks are not welcome to apply for the housing. The standard adopted for interpreting the advertisements is that of the ordinary reader "neither the most suspicious nor the most insensitive of our citizenry".

The court rejected the argument of the *New York Times* that if the plaintiffs were successful, this would require racially-conscious decisions in advertising and racial quotas in advertising. All that was required was that in constructing advertising images, advertisers should be careful to avoid the suggestion of a racial preference. Including a black model in order to avoid a charge of indicating a racial preference, was far removed from issues of racial quotas in hiring and education. The court also gave short shrift to arguments that this statute impinges on freedom of speech since the advertisements further an illegal activity, namely racial discrimination in the sale or rental of real estate.

The decision is somewhat limited by the standard of the ordinary consumer, the reasonable person, since it requires a reading from the position of the dominant common sense rather than from the viewpoint of the excluded group. The *New York Times* case dealt with a well documented claim of discrimination over 20 years and the courts have been more hesitant to find discrimination in relation to a limited number of advertisements. Again, this may reflect both an unwillingness to read the individual advertisement against the broader cumulative background and history of racist images[67] and a view of the issues as concerning a discrete image and its impact.

---

[66] (1991) 923 F.2d. 995. (2d. Circuit, Court of Appeal 1991).
[67] See *Housing Opportunities Made Equal v. Cincinnati Enquirer, Inc.* 943 F.2d. 644 (1991) and discussion in R. Robinson, "The Racial Limits of the Fair Housing Act: The Intersection of Dominant White Images, the Violence of Neighborhood Purity, and the Master Narrative of Black inferiority" (1995) 37 *William and Mary Law Review* 69.

(3) Sex-role stereotyping

The critique of sex-role stereotyping in the advertising media is a significant aspect of feminist critiques of the media. Trimble defines a stereotype as:

> "rigid and oversimplified generalizations of masculinity and femininity based on the assumption that males and females, by virtue of their sex, possess distinct psychological traits and characteristics. Stereotypes are manifested in broadcasting by portrayals of men and women that differ in the portrayal of their appearance, abilities, personality, power, occupation, and status."[68]

The women's movement argued in the 60s and 70s that existing advertising images showed women as "foolish creatures interested only in detergents, floor wax, shampoos, dog food and the like".[69] These stereotypes reinforced women's position in the private sphere and hampered their entry to and progression within the public sphere. Changing the images of women in the media was, therefore, one part of attempting to change social relations and the role of women in the public sphere. Advertising stereotypes were a conservative force within society holding back equality for women. Reformers argued that the media should simply portray women realistically "as free human beings with the same capacities as men".[70]

The current self-regulatory guidelines in Canada on sex-role stereotyping indicate that "[t]hese guidelines are designed to help creators of advertising develop positive images of women and eliminate systemic discrimination based on gender."[71] Prohibitions on unfair stereotyping now exist in many advertising codes and in Scandinavian Marketing Practices legislation. The Norwegian Marketing Control Act states that:

> "The advertiser and anyone who creates advertising shall ensure that the advertisement does not conflict with the inherent equality between the sexes

---

[68] L. Trimble, "Coming Soon to A Station Near You? The CRTC Policy on Sex-Role Stereotyping" in *Seeing Ourselves: Media Power and Policy in Canada* (E. Holmes and D. Taras eds. 1992), pp. 135–136.

[69] Quotations from women's groups submissions to the Canadian Royal Commission on the Status of Women in L. Trimble, "Coming Soon to A Station Near You; The Process and Impact of The Canadian Radio-Television and Telecommunication Commission's Involvement in Sex-Role Stereotyping" (Ph.D. Thesis, Queen's University, Kingston Ontario, 1990) p. 151.

[70] *ibid.*, p. 152.

[71] *Gender Portrayal Guidelines*, Canadian Advertising Foundation, (1994).

and that it does not imply any derogatory judgment of either sex or portray a man or a woman in an offensive manner."

There have undoubtedly been changes in the content of advertising since the sex-role stereotyping critique. It is difficult to measure the overall impact of these changes on gender equality. Measures such as the level of spousal abuse, rapes, or changes in material equality for women could be used but it would be difficult to draw any causal connections between advertising images and these measures. The controversy over pornography and its impact indicate the limitations of social science in measuring the impact of images on behaviour. There is of course an assumption in the critique of sex-role stereotyping that the demeaning images had effects in society.

Sex-role stereotyping guidelines seem to be relatively successful in addressing obviously offensive advertising such as the use of scantily clad women where there is no connection between the portrayal of a woman and the product advertised. Regulators do not have difficulty with sanctioning this conduct or the aggressive portrayal of women as sex-objects.[72] They appear to have difficulties with advertisements which partially rely on humour or where the advertisements are more subtle or abstract, giving rise to several possible interpretations. These are seen as raising matters of opinion and taste with the regulator viewed by critics as imposing their views of the advertisements over the views of the advertiser.

There are certain limitations to the stereotyping critique of advertising. First, there is the ability of advertising to co-opt the cultural values of feminism and associate them with commodities. Many advertisers reacted to feminism by taking its values, such as greater control over one's body, personal freedom and equality of treatment in the labour market, and associating these values with products.[73] Being in control and fighting off a hostile environment are common themes in contemporary cosmetic advertisements. Van Zoonen argues that the "new woman" often represents therefore a myth of progress since

---

[72] See S. Sverdrup and Eivind Sto, "Regulation of Sex Discrimination in Advertising: An Empirical Inquiry into the Norwegian Case" (1992) *Journal of Consumer Policy* 371 at 380. See also "Chauvinistic Advertising: decision of Consumer Ombudsman" (1995) *Consumer Law Journal* CS11.

[73] See the interesting discussion of this topic in R. Goldman, "Commodity Feminism" in *Reading Ads Socially* (1992), p. 130.

advertising co-opts feminist ideals into "acceptable fantasies of individual middle class achievement and success".[74] The fact that a woman is shown in a working environment does not mean that the advertisement does not continue to tap into the oppressive "male gaze" as argued by Wolf.

I noted in Chapter 2 that Naomi Wolf argues that a new stereotype has been created which is an oppressively normalising form of discourse. She maintains that women who do not conform face personal embarrassment or risk losing promotion because they are too fat or look too old. This phenomenon represents the intersection of consumer capitalism, which more and more rapidly transforms cultural signs into commodities, and deep cultural assumptions about gender and the female body. This system has been described as the "fashion-beauty complex". The power of this system does not depend on the false consciousness of women. Women may know that this system is oppressive, but like the "self-regulating subject" of Foucault, continually adjust their behaviour to these norms. The enormous growth in cosmetic surgery may represent some of these complexities of structure and agency in modern culture.[75] Women who undertake cosmetic surgery are not passive cultural dopes. They may do so reluctantly and with ambivalence, knowing that this potentially painful treatment is one which may allow them greater power over others within the confines of the existing system of gender relations. The fact that they may seem to gain more power does not detract from the systematic oppressiveness of the culture where such surgery is undertaken within particular normalising ideas of beauty. They are rarely undertaken to assert ethnic differences but to correct distortions from homogenising Anglo-Saxon norms of beauty.[76]

A second problem with the stereotyping critique is that it sometimes relies on the contrast between images of women and the realities of women's lives. There is value in pointing to these disparities but the critique does depend on the existence of a "reality" of women's lives. The reality of women's lives is a complex construct and would include among others, straight, black middle-class women, working-class lesbians, and single parents. Much post-modern work has critiqued the

---

[74] L. van Zoonen, *Feminist Media Studies* (1994), p. 72.
[75] See Bordo *loc. cit.*, and see Kathy Davis, "Remaking the She-Devil: A Critical Look at Feminist Approaches to Beauty" (1991) 6 *Hypatia* 21.
[76] Bordo *op. cit.*

idea of fixed identities of gender or race. Even if advertising does represent these differences it is likely to construct them as life-styles, as subjects for commodification and co-optation. Oppositional cultures may be co-opted and appropriated, just as the clothing industry in North America appropriated the culture of black urban youth in selling images of coolness in jeans and other clothing to white suburban youth (who had the income to buy these commodities).

Sex-role stereotyping is a valuable critique of advertising but needs to be situated within a theory of gender and race oppression and related to other issues of material inequality for women. Without these connections there is the danger that changes in images do little to address continuing inequalities, and merely dampen the development of critiques of consumer capitalism. The relative success of sex-role stereotyping critiques can be partly attributed to the fact that it is amenable to traditional forms of policy analysis such as a reliance on quantitative content analysis. Empirical and quantitatives studies could be undertaken of the difference between image and reality, the changes in the portrayal of women and the use of women in advertising roles, such as providing voice-overs in advertising. Policy-makers prefer hard data and the data can be used to provide clear benchmarks for success. This approach does have the potential, therefore, to bring pressure for greater diversity of presentation of men and women in the media and it can be used for long scale analyses which indicate the devaluation of particular groups in the media.

(4) Advertising as Pornography?

One of the most controversial issues in recent feminist literature is that of pornography. Carol Smart writes that there are two main approaches in feminism to this issue, "pornography-as-violence" and "pornography-as-representation".[77] The latter developed out of work on images of women in film and advertising. A common ground of these two positions is that "pornography eroticizes domination". However, pornography as representation, by focusing on techniques of representation and forms of discourse about women, emphasises the continuities in the pornographic genre which may not only be found in "traditional" forms of pornography but in advertising and Mills and Boon romances. Advertising

---

[77] C. Smart, *Feminism and the Power of Law* (1989) p. 116.

also uses similar techniques to pornography such as the "the pose" and "blocking", *i.e.* slowly showing the body in discrete blocks as an object rather than as a person.

In several imaginative essays Rosalind Coward[78] demonstrates the pornographic form in a number of different settings and the manner in which they contribute to women's oppression. She does not argue that oppression arises from a simple and forcible imposition of false needs on women. It is rather a complicated matter of the way in which oppression is produced in everyday life and how "female desire is constantly lured by discourses which sustain male privilege".[79] In one essay entitled "Naughty but Nice: Food Pornography" she examined advertisements for food in women's magazines. These elaborate images of rich foods promise, like, pornography, illicit pleasure since women are under constant pressure to control their body weight. Moreover, the food in the magazines is usually an exaggerated mock up, similar to the glamorous pictures of models, which will have been brushed and touched up to remove any blemishes. Women are the addressees of these advertisements and the consumption of food is tied to women's subordination in society since it is women who are generally involved in the preparation of food for others and who may be punished for indulging in this illicit activity through infringing the norms of the ideal body. To the extent that women actively recognise themselves and "buy in" to these advertisements they are reproducing patriarchal norms. Just as sexual pornography, through its regimes of representation, confirms male power over women, so food pornography:

"indulges a pleasure which is linked to servitude and therefore confirms the subordinate position of women ... The way images of food are made and circulated is not just innocent catering for pleasures. They also meddle in people's sense of themselves and their self–worth. In a sexually divided and hierarchical society, these pleasures are tied to positions of power and subordination".[80]

Coward's work emphasises the subtlety of the processes of representation at work in these advertisements, and their anchoring in social and cultural regimes of domination. Because much of the reading of the

---

[78] Rosalind Coward, *Female Desires* (1985).
[79] *ibid.*, at 16.
[80] *ibid.*, at 103, 106.

advertisement will be done without thinking, it is not difficult to understand why many individuals might overlook the significant ideological importance of the cumulation of these everyday interpretations intersecting with dominant cultural norms. The issue here is not a simple one of manipulation of the innocent by the power of advertising.

For those who conceive of pornography as representation, a major concern is the growing dominance of this pornographic form of representation, whether in traditional forms, or in advertising or Mills and Boon romances,[81] so that any alternative discourse of erotica is silenced. There are difficult questions of strategy here, whether to turn to the law to attack these images, to attempt to develop alternative voices in the mainstream or alternative media, or conduct graffiti campaigns or boycotts. The potentially wide scope of pornography as representation does raise difficult questions for bringing about social change through the law and Smart raises the question whether, given the difficulties of access to the media to develop alternative stories, it is "a valid feminist strategy ... to use the law to restrict certain images, even if this does not ensure the circulation of alternatives."[82]

In North America, the anti-pornography movement has used both criminal and civil law to attack pornographic images of women[83] and in the Canadian case of R. v. Butler[84] was successful in convincing the Supreme Court of Canada that pornography caused harm to women. This case concerned the prosecution of a bookseller under criminal obscenity provisions which prohibited the undue exploitation of sex. A traditional standard for obscenity had been that of community moral standards of tolerance. In Butler the standard was transformed to that of harm to groups in society. Sopinka J. held that pornography is harmful not because it offended against morality and might result in moral corruption, but because it was perceived by public opinion to be harmful to society by portraying women in positions of subordination, submission or humiliation. Pornography was proscribed because it offended principles of equality and dignity and predisposed persons to mistreat women. Social science evidence before the court of the link

[81] Smart op. cit. at p. 125: See also M. Valverde, Sex Power and Pleasure (1985).
[82] Smart op. cit. at p. 128.
[83] Although feminist groups did succeed in introducing legislation, this was struck down in American Booksellers v. Hudnut 771 F.2d. 323 (7th Circuit, 1985) affirmed 475 U.S. (1986).
[84] [1992] 1 S.C.R. 452.

between obscenity and harm was limited but the court thought it reasonable to assume that "exposure to images bears a causal relationship to changes in attitudes and beliefs".[85]

The representations of pornography were proscribed partly because they portrayed women "as a class as objects for sexual exploitation and abuse [and] have a negative impact on the individual's sense of self-worth and acceptance"[86] and the majority referred to an earlier report which had argued that pornography reinforced male-female stereotypes. This critique could of course be applied to much advertising, as has been noted in critiques of sex role stereotyping and of images of black female sexuality in advertising posters. One of the major themes of advertising in consumer capitalism has been the sexualisation of commodities and writers such as Naomi Wolf argue that the advertising of the 1980s adopted the conventions of high-class pornography in its representations of women. Catherine Mackinnon has noted that "[m]any in my audiences appear convinced that ads do a lot more damage to women than even the most violent pornography. This is because ads are more legitimate, more pervasive, more artistic, and show more recognizable violence..."[87]

The fact that advertising uses similar photographic techniques to pornography does not necessarily mean that advertising should be equated with pornography. To do so would be to adopt a formalistic approach, ignoring the differing social and cultural context of the production and consumption of advertising and pornography.

Since the *Butler* case in Canada, there appears to have been an increase in moral policing, particularly of gay and lesbian bookstores. This raises the concern that critiques of cultural oppression become entwined with more conservative movements for moral policing or the protection of family values, which are abhorred by representations which stray beyond vanilla sex. Sopinka J., for example, is a conservative judge who opposed regulation of tobacco advertising as an unwarranted intrusion on freedom of commercial speech, but needed little convincing of the "common sense" arguments in *Butler* concerning pornography.

---

[85] Sopinka J. at 502.
[86] *ibid.*, at 497.
[87] C. MacKinnon *Feminism Unmodified* (1987), p. 223.

Summary

There is a developing jurisprudence in relation to unfair advertising images in both court decisions, administrative decision-making and soft law. These developments may be based on human rights concepts of equality, recognising the cultural power of images to reproduce oppress-ive images of groups which have been historically disadvantaged. Regulation of harmful advertising images does not encounter, to the same extent, the same problems as regulation of other aspects of speech. It is unlikely to be used to attack the powerless or those who challenge conventional values as is the danger with regulation of pornography. It is, in general, regulating relatively powerful business interests. The jurisprudence is developing slowly and still lacks coherence. Decision-makers have greater confidence in addressing the apparently outrageous advertisement, for example, where women are portrayed as sexual objects or where the woman portrayed has no connection to the product being sold. There is a consensus in soft law and administrative decisions on these issues.

The more difficult issues are attacking the routine and more subtle racist and gendered stereotypes in advertising. The *Butler* decision indicates the potential in the concept of harm rather than community offensiveness as a basis for regulation. This involves interpretive judg-ments about the relationship between images and harm but these issues are not merely matters of opinion or taste. They may be subjective in the sense that there is not a correct answer. There is no moral meter bar. But most legal judgments are of this nature. Assistance could be sought in interpretive theories which relate advertising images to the narratives of racism and sexism. This requires the decision-maker to reflect on historically embedded stereotypes and the extent to which the advertisement reproduces and recycles these stereotypes. This approach could provide a critical cultural challenge to common sense, in the sense of routine understandings. This may involve a rejection of "the ordinary reader" test since the decision-maker is not solely concerned with how the current ordinary reader might understand the advertisement it but how one might interpret the advertisement in the light of a critical reflection on whether it reproduces stereotypes of historically disadvantaged groups.

It is not easy to challenge common sense ideas which sustain inequality and domination. The development of arguments of harm from images raises the role of differing forms of knowledge in the policy process. The preference for hard knowledge in many regulatory areas means that it may be difficult to convince decision-makers through interpretive theories of harm which are not based on empirical data. Yet issues of cultural harm from images inevitably raise questions of interpretive knowledge. They implicate public values of equality and dignity, issues upon which the courts are assumed in many countries to have expertise. Some writers are pessimistic about any strategy to use courts to challenge dominant common sense.[88] These questions are partly cultural, related to the role of courts in different countries. It may be possible, therefore, that the courts may be a source of symbolic contests over values, and the *Butler* decision is evidence of this. The criticisms of the *Butler* decision suggest that the courts may not always make the right decisions and that other strategies, boycotts, graffiti campaigns, alternative media may be more effective. There is not, however, an *a priori* answer to this question.

---

[88] See R. Delgado and J. Stefancic, "Minority Men, Misery and the Marketplace of Ideas" in M. Berger, B. Wallis and S. Watson, eds. *Constructing Masculinity* (1995) pp. 211–220.

Chapter 5

Conclusion

This study of advertising concerns the intersection of market power with cultural classifications and normalising discourses under consumer capitalism. Advertising is part of a sophisticated system of corporate communications and public relations behaviour that is embedded within and acts upon contemporary culture. Controlling its cultural effects— pervasive commercialism, the impact of the secondary images of advertising in their depictions of groups and desirable social relationships, and advertising's contribution to cultural domination by corporate values—is a significant challenge for law and regulation. The challenge is made more acute by the increasing concentration of commercial media conglomerates and the direct and indirect control of advertising interests over the form and content of the media.

The power of advertising to shape consciousness fuels concerns about the democratic control of advertising, the media and the management of meaning in society. The commercial media and public relations have seeped into all aspects of life, raising questions about the relationship between a market economy based on the principles of consumer capitalism and a democratic culture.[1] Corporate influence over the media is a phenomenon commonplace in the USA and of increasing concern in the United Kingdom and elsewhere. The "citizen as consumer" thesis suggests that the pervasive commercialism of the media has undermined democratic culture so that societies have become "Consumer Culture Inc."[2]

This chapter recaps the central issues concerning the power of

---

[1] See S. Kline and W. Leiss, "The Ravelled Sleeve: Advertising Policy in Canada" in H. Holmes and D. Taras eds, *Seeing Ourselves: Media Power and Policy* (1992), p. 121.
[2] See H. Schiller, *Culture Inc.* (1989).

advertising raised in this book. It also suggests some rethinking of legal analysis of advertising messages and images and examines possible approaches to regulation of the ground rules of advertising.

1 Advertising, Consumption and Democracy

There are three standard defences to attacks on the power of advertising images and criticisms that they may be unfair and exploitative. First, advertising merely reflects society.

"Ads have to portray life in a form in which the people for whom they are written will recognise it. An ad is not a thesis on what society might be like under different or changed circumstances: it is simply a tool for selling products to people as they are now ... it is not the role of advertising to change society. Nor could it do so if it tried".[3]

The second argument is that if individuals do not like advertising for products then they can exercise their vote in the market. Finally, the cure for unfair advertising, namely government regulation, is worse than the disease.

Commercial advertising is not simply information as suggested by the ideology of the commercial speech doctrine. Nor is advertising merely an attempt to sell products. Culture and economy are inextricably linked in the marketplace of consumer capitalism through the mechanism of advertising. Advertising carries messages about social relations and it makes implicitly authoritative statements about normal behaviour, comparisons with others, inclusion and exclusion. Its appropriation and compression of images into stereotypes, "tosses ambivalence and ambiguity—that is the stuff that life is made of—out of the window."[4] The bottom line remains that of product consumption as a central part of life.

Consumers are not passive receivers of advertising messages, as suggested by some theorists, but they are invited continually to view as

[3] R. White and J. Lannon, "Advertising and Society" in *The Case for Advertising* (J. Walter Thompson, ed., 1976) p. 10 quoted in N. Smith, *Morality and the Market: Consumer Pressure for Corporate Accountability* (1990) p. 312, n. 10.
[4] L. Savan, *The Sponsored Life: Ads TV and American Culture* (1994), p. 215.

commonsense the images of social relations in advertising. To the extent that they automatically make the connections within the advertisement as part of everyday common sense, they are acting on and reproducing the images. Advertisements are not mere reflections but play a constitutive role in individuals' conceptions of themselves and their social relationships. Interpretation of and resistance to the secondary meanings in advertising by consumers is a political site for struggle over the management of meaning in society. This richer view of the relationship between structure and agency in social life suggests a need to adjust the simple dichotomies in existing public policies between free choice and government paternalism.

That consumers continue to buy the products advertised does not necessarily mean that they agree with the secondary messages in advertisements. Consider, for example, the findings of a 1994 study of women's responses to advertising.[5] Nine out of 10 respondents think that women are influenced by media portrayal of women and that media images which reinforce the idea that women must be thin to be beautiful are troubling. Almost three-quarters of those surveyed indicated that they had talked with friends about advertising which concerned them but only eight per cent had written letters of complaint. More than half had silently boycotted companies whose advertising they found offensive. This final finding seems to support in part the argument that the market will punish offensive advertising. More telling, however, is the fact that despite significant disquiet about the advertising very few individuals had complained.

The typical response of industry to such findings is that consumer boycotts would be a serious concern, but that consumer objections to images should not function to censor the creative process of advertising.[6] This almost proprietary response illustrates O'Barr's view that complaints about the secondary images of advertising "threaten the management of meaning that the producers of cultural ideas feel is rightly theirs. At issue is the determination of one's ideas of self, of society and of others".[7]

The study demonstrates that lack of complaints does not indicate assent to secondary meanings in advertisements. The consumers who were surveyed had resisted the images in the advertisements. But

---

[5] Media Watch, "Please Adjust Our Sets-Canadian Women Watching Television" (1994).
[6] This point is made by W. O'Barr in *Culture and the Ad* (1994), p. 204.
[7] O'Barr, *ibid.*, p. 205.

advertising will probably find a method of repackaging the image of the concerned woman who is concerned about social issues and therefore buys Brand X.

Is there any reason to focus criticism on advertising rather than other forms of media images in films, TV and other forms? Advertising is important because it is among the most high-profile aspects of the media system that plays such a significant role in the management of meaning in society. It is a powerful force in the lives of many consumers. Critiques of advertising are fundamentally attempts to understand "who is in charge and how they manage their power over others".[8]

Advertising is also the quintessential post-modern form. Jameson argues that a central aspect of post-modern thought is "depthlessness". This refers to the repudiation of distinctions which were part of modernism, such as the distinction between appearance and essence and between the authentic and the alienated subject.[9] The post-modern critique of "fixed identities" with its image of the free-floating consumer within a sea of discourses is an example of the rejection of these dichotomies. Depthlessness refers also, however, to a more fundamental flattening of time and reconfiguration of space. Electronic images flatten history into visual mirages and stereotypes. The new global space becomes a site for media images which rely often on stereotypes. Edward Said describes the way in which other cultures are presented on U.S. television:

"The history of other cultures is non-existent until it erupts into confrontation with the United States; most of what counts about foreign societies is compressed into thirty-second sound bites, and into the question of whether they are pro- or anti-America, freedom, capitalism, democracy".[10]

Advertising compresses and reproduces these stereotypes. History in advertising becomes nostalgia for a simpler world or a pastiche of clichés.

The third argument against regulation is that the cure is worse than the disease. In a thoughtful article written in 1970 Michael Trebilcock documented the pervasive power of advertising and argued that we seemed to be faced with the need to chart a course between the Scylla

[8] *ibid.*, at 203.
[9] F. Jameson, *Post-Modernism or The Cultural Logic of Late Capitalism* (1991) pp. 6, 12.
[10] E. Said, *Culture and Imperialism* (1993), p. 323.

of the corporate planned good life and the Charybdis of a state planned good life.[11] His solution was a philosophy of information. Since he wrote that article, it might be argued that there has been greater movement in the direction of a corporate planned good life than a state-planned life. In most countries the state both as provider of goods and services and as a welfare state has retreated, but establishing the ground rules for consumer markets does not necessarily imply a state-planned good life. It does require analysis of what type of market structure should be encouraged, which is as much a cultural as an economic question.

An issue which must be faced is whether critiques of advertising are drawing attention away from "real" social issues such as the implications for communities of the structural changes in capital, the poor conditions of labour which produce the consumer products, and the material problems faced by poor consumers. The high visibility of advertising makes it not so much a scapegoat as a sitting duck.[12] Similar critiques might be made of feminist campaigns in relation to pornography or the portrayal of women's sexuality in advertising. They are high-profile but may draw attention away from issues such as improving job prospects and welfare facilities for women.[13] The fact that women have higher levels of economic and social equality in countries which are more tolerant of pornography raises questions about this strategy.[14]

There is some force in these criticisms but advertising may be one site for developing criticisms of consumer capitalism. It can act also as a catalyst for analysis of the connections between material economic relations and culture. The images of advertising deny the reality of the conditions of production of the products advertised and many of the realities of social divisions based on race, gender and class. Critiques of advertising may be, therefore, a link in a broader critique. At the same time, there is the danger of confusing serious critiques—with the outrages of middle-class or conservative moralities and moral panics.

---

[11] M. Trebilcock, "Consumer Protection in the Affluent Society" (1970) 16 *McGill L.J.* 263.
[12] See M. Schudson, *Advertising: The Uneasy Persuasion* (1984), p. 8 cited in J. Sinclair, *Images Incorporated: Advertising as Industry and Ideology* (1987), p. 183.
[13] L. Segal, "Does Pornography Cause Violence? The Search for Evidence" in P.C. Gibson and R. Gibson (eds.) *Dirty Looks: Women, Pornography, Power* (1993), p. 17.
[14] *ibid.*, at p. 18 citing L. Baron, "Pornography and Gender Equality: An Empirical Analysis" (1990) 27:3 *Journal of Sex Research.*

2 Towards An Expanded Vocabulary of Advertising Law

Consumer law has focused primarily on the instrumental role of law in addressing market failures or redistributing rights and resources to consumers. This role of law in addressing material inequality in the position of the consumer is important. But the law, like advertising, also plays a role in constituting the legal subject of consumer relations and this is of ideological significance. Consumer law may be viewed as having developed initially as a critique of the abstract, free and equal subject of classical contract law. It represented an attempt by liberal law to adjust the law to the realities of the social relations of consumer capitalism.

The subject of consumer law reflects however the structures of its origins in liberal legal thought. The legal consumer was originally constructed as an exception to the market norm of behaviour. S/he was often constructed as an innocent[15] or victim. This subject has been constructed around hierarchical dualisms of liberal legal thought such as the reasonable and the credulous, the former sometimes being associated with supposed male virtues of rationality, while the credulous consumer is irrational and female.[16] However, gender is not the only social relationship that is implicated. The legal subject "consumer" is a cultural construction which depends on the continuing construction of "the other" as lacking the characteristics of the rational, carefully choosing consumer. The other may be children,[17] racial minorities,[18]

---

[15] In a standard U.S. text the author argues in the introduction that, although commercial and consumer law overlap there is a difference in the relevant standards. He cites to the following quotation from the Supreme Judicial Court of Massachussetts: "[Perhaps] a different standard applies to transactions between two worldly wise businesses and a ... consumer who is not inured to the rough and tumble of the world of commerce ... One can easily imagine cases where an act might be unfair if practiced upon a commercial innocent yet would be common practice between two people engaged in business". *Spence v. Boston Edison Co.* 390 Mass. 604, 616 (1983) cited in M. Greenfield, *Consumer Law: A Guide for Those Who Represent Sellers, Lenders, and Consumers* (1995), p. 4.
[16] See F. Olsen, "The Sex of Law" in *The Politics of law* (D. Kairys ed. 1990), p. 453.
[17] See *Irwin Toy, op. cit.*
[18] See the discussion of *Williams v. Walker Thomas Furniture Co.* in M. Spence, (1993–94) *Temple Political and Civil Rights Law Review* 89, and see more generally K. Crenshaw, "Race, Reform and Retrenchment" (1988) Harv. L. R. 1331 at 1370–1381.

individuals from working class backgrounds,[19] or the elderly,[20] but these representations of "the other" are not innocent. They play a role in bolstering images of normality and the boundaries of behaviour, (don't behave like a child!) and they may sustain inequality and domination. To the extent that individuals see themselves through the lens of the dominant cultural construction they may blame their failings on themselves. They have failed to match up to the standard of the rational consumer and only merit protection through paternalism for the weak and vulnerable.

When consumer law developed in the 1960s it was a modest attempt to recognise the position of "the other" in the law and act as a critique of the irrationalities and exploitation which characterised some of the central practices of consumer capitalism, such as artificial product differentiation,[21] the fact that the poor pay more for basic needs,[22] the environmental costs of consumption[23] and the ideological impact of advertising on equality and conceptions of social priorities.[24] These critiques often raised questions of class, gender and race.

The law has transformed these critiques into a legal common sense where problems are individualised within the dichotomous image of the rational (normal) consumer and the vulnerable (or credulous) consumer. This approach is not merely model building but is taken to be an unproblematic representation of a world in which inequalities of social class, gender and race do not exist. The influence of law and economics on consumer law has exacerbated this method of thought. The abstract "rational consumer" used in economic model building is mistaken for and mingled with a cultural vision of the reasonable consumer. As a consequence, the law of consumer relations is often more focused on the rationality or irrationality of the consumer, than the selling practices of consumer capitalism. The issue becomes whether to provide exceptional and paternalistic protection for the irrational or

---

[19] See the Canadian case of *Trans Canada Credit v. Zaluski* [1969] 20.R.496.
[20] See *Dominion Home Improvements v. Knuude Ont.* D.C. (unreported, 1986) in J. Ziegal, B. Geva and R. Cuming, *Commercial and Consumer Transactions* (3rd ed., 1995) vol. 1, p. 75.
[21] See discussion earlier at pp. 31–32.
[22] The classic remains D. Caplovitz, *The Poor Pay More* (1963).
[23] R. Carson, *Silent Spring* (1963). For a current analysis of the impact of consumption on the world's resources see A. Durning, *How Much is Enough* (1992).
[24] One of the best critiques here is J.K. Galbraith, *The Affluent Society* (4th ed., 1984) and see Ellen Willis, "Consumerism and Women" in *Woman in Sexist Society* (V. Gornick and K. Moran eds., 1971).

vulnerable consumer, while the central core of consumer law is the provision of information to the rational consumer. The law of commercial speech has provided a constitutional underpinning for this common sense.

The doctrine of commercial speech is a Trojan horse of commercial interests. It is portrayed as a consumerist measure with its focus on information for consumers and "listeners' rights". Its contribution to consumer protection, however, is far outweighed by its use by corporate interests. Moreover, traditional arguments for protecting free speech do not justify constitutional protection of corporate advertising.

The structure of much judicial thought concerning the regulation of commercial speech is ideological in the traditional meaning of that term: a false conception of reality. Since all market structures, and market cultures, are an artefact of an existing complex of legal permissions and prohibitions, it is incoherent to pit "freedom" against "intervention". Yet this purported contest is at the heart of judicial rhetoric. "Free markets" are associated with an absence of control over advertising and government regulation with intervention in the market. The ideological conception of the legal subject as the unsituated but informed consumer is used to justify deregulation and a preference for information remedies over standards.

Exposing the ideological underpinnings of legal thought does not solve the problem of regulation but it suggests that we need to go beyond the *a priori* and rather formalistic approach of existing legal rhetoric. Rejection of commercial speech protection for advertising does not involve a rejection of markets or acceptance of the belief that government regulation of consumer markets is always beneficial to consumers. It simply indicates that these are issues which should not be put beyond democratic politics through constitutional entrenchment of a particular cultural vision.

The standard of the credulous consumer or the "consumer as idiot" in misleading advertising has often been associated with supposedly feminine characteristics. Yet this construction has ignored the actual social situation of many women, such as the fact that they have acted, and continue to act, as the careful unpaid managers of households, a job requiring complex skills.[25] The social effacement of this role is

---

[25] See Cynthia Wright, "Feminine Trifles of Vast Importance": Writing Gender into the History of Consumption" in *Gender Conflicts: New Essays in Women's History* (F. Iacovetta and M. Valverde, eds., 1992) p. 229.

nowhere more evident than in legal constructions of the feminine consumer. By bringing these social facts back into the analysis, legal decision-makers would be required to rethink their assumptions. Similarly, criticism of the overdrawn contrast between the rational adult and the manipulated child in the decision of the Supreme Court of Canada in *Irwin Toy* raises questions about the supposed rationality of many consumption decisions.

One person's credulity is another person's trust, and trust is viewed by many writers as an important prerequisite of commercial transactions. Law and regulation may be of particular significance in affecting the cultural norms of market behavior, playing a constitutive role in establishing the ground rules of markets. The concept of truth in advertising has been criticised as an outmoded objective in the postmodern world of signs and symbolic gratification, and the goal of truth is portrayed sometimes as a literal-minded puritanism. Truth in advertising may be viewed, however, as an important step towards achieving a norm of trust in consumer markets. This is recognised in relation to such markets as the sale of securities where the emphasis is not on the irrationality of consumers but on the importance of maintaining confidence in the market institution. This aspect of regulation has been neglected in relation to general consumer markets. Thus the sale of automobiles continues to involve cultural rituals that would never be tolerated for the sale of stocks in the stock market. One technique for disrupting the reasonable/credulous distinction is to draw attention to this difference and query why regulation should be so much more solicitous of the interests of the generally white middle-class males who trade in this market rather than the ordinary consumer purchasing an automobile. Another, perhaps equally compelling attack on the distinction is to highlight the "normal" irrationality of those whom the law portrays as "reasonable". Thus Duncan Kennedy argues that the white middle-class males who gamble on the stock exchange are just as irrational as the ordinary consumer and that their protection is justified on paternalistic grounds.[26]

There is a greater need to recognise the constitutive role of advertising law. This understanding of the law can be seen most clearly in the case of commercial speech since it is commonplace to view constitutional

---

[26] D. Kennedy, "Distributive and Paternalist Motives in Contract and Tort Law With Special Reference to Compulsory Terms and Unequal Bargaining Power" (1981–82) 41 *Maryland Law Review* 563.

cases as embodying cultural and political choices. But legal distinctions between "puffs" and actionable misrepresentation claims reflect cultural understandings of the role and power of images and representations. The law of sex role stereotyping and discriminatory advertising reflects clearly assumptions about the cultural power of images.

Cases and commentaries on advertising law make assumptions about how reasonable consumers would understand advertising images and claims. This reasonable person will often be constructed through the lens of middle-class white judges who will rarely have management of everyday consumption decisions. These judges were once lawyers and Stewart Macaulay, in his study of lawyers and consumer protection laws, found that they were often not sympathetic to consumer cases. This was not solely because of the economics of legal practice but because most lawyers appeared to have assimilated the dominant norms of consumer capitalism—that it is important to read one's contract and so on. Consumer clients were often constructed as aberrational characters.[27]

Given the general position and background of the judiciary there is likely to be a tendency to view issues of reasonableness through the lens of the dominant public culture. This permits occasional protection for the weak and disapproval of the outrageous. But a major question is whether the courts can be convinced to look at issues of interpretation through the lens of the victims of cultural domination, or at least to understand the contributions of routine cultural images and practices to disempowerment. Attempts to do so might draw on approaches to discrimination law which indicate the importance of understanding workplace practices from the viewpoint of the victim rather than the reasonable person.[28]

There are certain existing conventions for legal interpretation of advertising messages. The "puff" is to be distinguished from the factual statements; deception is a separate category from unfairness. When the going gets tough in interpreting advertising texts we may turn to empirical surveys. There is an assumption that judges are making factual judgments so that if we had enough empirical evidence available it would confirm or falsify their judgment as to whether a claim was understood as a mere puff or a factual claim. But if we return to Mr

---

[27] S. Macaulay, "Lawyers and Consumer Protection Law" (1979–80) 14 *Law and Society Review* 115.
[28] See discussion in Chap. 4, p. 122.

Overton's suit in relation to his failed fantasies in relation to Bud Light in Chapter 2, it could be said that the judge made a political judgment that the potential harm from the failed fantasy was not a harm recognised by the law. It is quite possible that some consumers do in fact believe that consuming this beer may identify them as more attractive.

The issue in the case was not factual but normative. It is important to view advertising law through a normative lens. Courts are not merely making factual determinations but political choices concerning the public values of the market and whose vision of common sense is made to stick in society. Many writers, particularly in the USA, have argued that the use of positivistic social science would aid decision-makers in difficult cases such as those involving alleged exploitation of consumer emotions or artificial product differentiation. Social science studies would assess the harm from such practices. However, assessing the harm from advertising images may not be a simple task. In the case of advertising to children and tobacco advertising, social science evidence did not provide a firm ground for policy-making and in relation to advertising to children may have obfuscated the cultural and political issues at stake over children's advertising.

An alternative is to focus on the normalising effects of images in advertising, a task involving interpretive judgment rather than empirical knowledge. Carol Smart quotes Robin Eckersley on the problem of proving "harm" caused by pornography:

> "The ... problem is that concentration [on] the effects of pornography at the behavioral level tends to deflect feminist analysis away from other types of 'effects' at an ideological level such as the way in which pornography contributes to the organization of the everyday viewing of women as a 'desirable commodity' to be consumed by men. The search for 'hard' empirical evidence operates to narrow not only the definition of the problem, but also the theoretical framework and the range of possible feminist strategies that might be employed".[29]

Empirical evidence is not, however, irrelevant. Data on sex-role stereo-

---

[29] R. Eckersley, "Whither the feminist campaign? An evaluation of feminist critiques of pornography" (1987) 15 *International Journal of the Sociology of Law* 149 at 163 quoted in C. Smart, *Feminism and the Power of Law* (1989), p. 127.

typing played a role in attacking images of women in advertising. It is merely one part of the analysis.

Social scientists have themselves begun to question the cultural biases of much marketing research which is often used as expert testimony in advertising cases.[30] A cultural/interpretive approach does not mean that one is simply engaged in unstructured debate as to the effects of advertising. Lawyers could develop theories of the cultural effects of particular advertising images based on the approaches outlined in Chapter 3. I suggested also in Chapter 4 how evidence concerning the normalising power of advertising might be developed in relation to images of women in advertising. There are, however, dangers and problems in any attempt to incorporate a cultural perspective into legal discourse. Law itself is a cultural discourse and cultural studies challenges law's construction of the subject as coherent, rational and autonomous. The alternative conception of the socially-situated subject is unlikely, therefore, to be accepted easily. Liberal legal thought has traditionally obscured structural influences—such as class, gender or race—in decision-making or attributions of responsibility. Arguments about cumulative cultural influences and their harm will face similar diffi-culties. The controversy over the battered woman's defence suggests hesitancy to recognise the effects of cultural subordination or to situate the rational subject in social structures. A further danger is that where the law has regulated images, as in the case of pornography, there is justified concern that such regulation is used to target those groups whose sexual expression differs from and challenges the dominant norms of heterosexual bourgeois values. The law has often acted as a censor of popular (particularly youth) culture as reflected in moral panics over such topics as crime comics.

Unlike obscenity, regulation of advertising images does not raise significant issues of censorship of creativity and is generally concerned with advertising by large corporate groups. It may be possible to focus on the issue of harm which is attributable to the circulation of the image, such as the association of cigarette consumption with desirable lifestyles. Even here however there are difficulties in framing clear rules, since the cigarette manufacturers have shown that they are able to subvert bans on lifestyle advertising. In order to be effective, regulation

---

[30] See J.M. Bristor and E. Fisher, "Feminist Thought: Implications for Consumer Research" (1993) *Journal of Consumer Research* 518.

of images may necessarily be required to be over-inclusive.

In contrast to consumer law, the law of trademark protection has taken images very seriously, recognising the importance of images as property. A number of companies include their product names (*e.g.* Guinness) as assets in their balance sheet.[31] The power of the "puff" is recognised here as an important property right entitled to protection. The holders of the property rights in brand images are able, through trademark law to prevent individuals "playing with the signs" through irony and parody.

Irony represents a central style of post-modernism. It is embodied in the active consumer playing with the slogans of consumer culture and the "resistive pleasures" of sub-cultures of consumption. Applied to advertising it suggests that the response to advertisements is the "knowing wink".[32] Consumers know the games of advertisers and find it amusing to play along, believing that they are ultimately in control. But the industry has struck back. Much contemporary advertising relies on irony to sell to the sophisticated or cool consumer audience.

Parody offers the potential for a more profound critique, but law constrains its potential. The signs and symbols of consumer culture such as Ronald McDonald are a central form of new property and are protected with an assiduousness reserved historically for precious state artefacts. In the U.S. these property rights have been used to trump free speech rights on the basis that alternative avenues of communication existed for parodying the product.[33]

The world of commodities has become a world of signs but the law seems currently to view these signs as a benign form of consumer information rather than cultural images which may be used as methods of artificial product differentiation. Recognition of consumption as idealist as well as a materialist practice suggests that artificial product differentiation should be restored to the policy agenda.

At a more general level recognition of the idealist nature of much consumption does not imply either blanket condemnation (consumers manipulated to believe that they get status from products) a distanced toleration of the masses (if the ordinary folk get pleasure from these

---

[31] See C. Lury, *Cultural Rights: Technology, Legality Personality* (1993), p. 9.

[32] See L. Savan, *The Sponsored Life* (1994) p. 6.

[33] See *Mutual of Omaha Insurance Co. v. Novak* 836 F.2d. 397 (1987). (Individual had produced "Mutant of Omaha" T-shirts parodying Mutual of Omaha Insurance company).

products then who are we to interfere) or an enthusiastic endorsement of "the compleat consumer" (achieving autonomy and identity through consumption). It should recognise however some of the potential implications of image advertising. There may be significant externalities from advertising's use of images and its continuing offer of changing or multiple identities to consumers. We have noted some of these: addictions to shopping, anorexia and bulimia, the potential impact on poor children excluded from the feast, continued reproduction of gender and racial stereotyping. Advertising cannot plead that it is innocent in relation to these effects.

Throughout this discussion I have been implicitly assuming the courts to be the interpreters of the law. But there may be other institutional frameworks which might provide the opportunity for developing norms and dialogue concerning advertising practices. These include the model of the U.S. regulatory agency, the quasi-public Advertising Standards Authority in the United Kingdom, and the Consumer Ombuds model in Scandinavia. The U.S. model depends for its legitimacy partly on the model of scientific expertise and is more likely to turn to scientific knowledge, such as social science, in developing regulation. It does not provide a great deal of opportunity for democratic dialogue and is subject to the legal rationality review of the courts. In contrast, the ASA may be more likened to an institution which provides a focus for discourse on advertising practices. The norms which develop are a form of soft law and are more flexible than legal provisions. The contribution of the public is, however, only through the complaint mechanism of voice and there is little opportunity for critical dialogue about advertising. The legislature is an obvious forum for discussion and control of advertising, but legislative attention tends to be sporadic.

One important conclusion is that there is little opportunity for development of critical public commentary on advertising practices and their effects. While the courts might have some impact here, they are not easily accessible and seem unsuited to provide a rich commentary on the everyday world of advertising images. Several further possibilities might be considered. Media literacy education is one obvious example. Others include measures which increase democratic dialogue by allowing greater opportunity to "talk back" to the messages in advertising, the use of boycotts and other forms of grassroots campaigns in relation to advertising messages and controlling the ground rules for advertising by capping commercial advertising expenditures.

RETHINKING LISTENERS' RIGHTS: TALKING BACK, FAIRNESS AND ITS LIMITS

A dominant rationale for protection of freedom of expression has been the marketplace of ideas. A common response to concerns about media domination or advertising stereotypes is that of "more speech" or facilitation of alternative speech. One model for facilitating this in a commercially dominated system is the fairness doctrine. In the U.S. this doctrine, based on the scarcity of the airwaves, required broadcasters to carry contrasting views on controversial matters of public importance. In its famous decision, *Red Lion Broadcasting v. FCC*[34], the Supreme Court viewed the fairness doctrine as furthering the marketplace of ideas, contributing to informed public opinion. In this case a radio station had broadcast, as part of a "Christian Crusade" series, an attack on the author of a book entitled "Goldwater-Extremist on the Right". The broadcast included a number of personal attacks on the author alleging that he was a communist and had been fired for fraudulent newspaper reporting. The station refused the author free reply time under the fairness doctrine and argued that the fairness doctrine challenged their right to broadcast whatever they wished. The court rejected the station's arguments, indicating that the fairness doctrine furthered the goals of the First Amendment. The airwaves were a democratic resource and "it is the right of the viewers and listeners, not the right of the broadcasters which is paramount". The court feared that without the fairness doctrine there could be a monopolisation of the market of ideas. Without it "station owners and a few networks would have unfettered power to make time available only to the highest bidders, to communicate only their own views on public issues ... There is no sanctuary in the First Amendment for unlimited private censorship operating in a medium not open to all."[35]

The fairness doctrine was applied to cigarette advertising in a ruling of the Federal Communications Commission which required radio and television stations which carried cigarette advertising to devote a significant amount of broadcast time to present the case against cigarette smoking.[36] The possibility of applying the doctrine more generally was raised in relation to advertising of high-powered, pollution causing

---

[34] 395 U.S. 367 (1969).
[35] *ibid.*, White J. at 1807.
[36] See discussion in *Banzhaf v. F.C.C.* 405 F.2d. 1082 (1969).

automobiles[37] and, in the early 1970s, the Federal Trade Commission argued that counter advertising should be permitted in relation to advertising which raised controversial issues of public importance such as pollution, nutrition, automobile safety or which encouraged the use of drugs to solve personal problems. They had argued that there should be limited access rights which would not reply to individual advertisements but which would present a counter-view to that implicitly or explicitly put forward in the advertisement.

The Federal Communications Commission in 1974 rejected the F.T.C. proposals and refused to extend the fairness doctrine beyond what it conceived to be the special case of cigarette advertising. The Commission drew a distinction between editorial advertising, such as advertising explicitly or implicitly advocating a position on a controversial issue of public importance such as abortion or the construction of the Alaska oil pipeline[38] and advertisements for products and services. The Commission rejected the application of the fairness doctrine to the latter, concluding that "we do not believe that the usual product commercial can realistically be said to inform the public on any side of a controversial issue of public importance".[39] This blanket rejection of the fairness doctrine to general product advertising avoided the difficulties of attempting to determine when advertising might implicitly raise questions of public importance. It is not difficult to critique the assumptions of the F.C.C. Almost all advertising on the broadcast media advocates the purchase of products, and has a continuing shaping effect on private and public culture. Environmental advertising suggests that the solution to the problem of sustainable consumption is through continued purchases of environmentally friendly products.

Two years later the Supreme Court provided constitutional protection to corporate product advertising because of its assumed contribution to the marketplace of ideas, an assumption denied by the Federal Communications Commission. It is ironic that in *Virginia Pharmacy* Blackmun J. justified the listeners' rights rationale for protection of commercial speech partly by reference to the decision of the court in *Red Lion*. Listeners' rights had been viewed as a mechanism for ensuring that the public would be exposed to a wide diversity of views. It was a

---

[37] See *Friends of the Earth v. F.C.C.* 449 F.2d. 1164 (1971).
[38] See Federal Communications Commission *Fairness Report* 48 F.C.C. 2d. 1 at 23.
[39] *ibid.*, p. 26.

substitute for the public service tradition associated with public broadcasting in the United Kingdom.[40]

The application of the fairness doctrine to product advertising challenged the power of control of private advertisers over the media. The cigarette counter-advertising was remarkably successful and the tobacco companies were happy to cease broadcasting on television. Conservative critics of the application of the fairness doctrine to advertising saw correctly that it challenged dominant corporate values and could undermine the economic basis of television financing through product advertising.[41] It was hardly surprising that the Federal Communications Commission, often regarded as an agency particularly prone to capture by broadcasting interests, would refuse to extend the fairness doctrine to product advertising.

Current wisdom suggests that there is little role for the fairness doctrine in broadcasting. The proliferation of channels and the growth of "narrow casting" is claimed to have undermined the scarcity rationale for regulation of broadcasting content. But there must remain disquiet. There is still significant advertising on many channels. The supposed diversity of current developments may lead to significant class distinctions between those viewing quality cable channels and those viewing network programming, which is dominated by entertainment. This could undermine any possibility of the electronic media providing a public culture which would encourage a critical engagement with public issues.[42] The counter-advertising strategy continues to be used in a number of countries where it is financed often by a modest tax on commercial advertising of products. In California a tax on tobacco products finances counter advertising in relation to tobacco.

The fairness doctrine is a modest possibility for alternative speech. However, the strategy of more speech as a solution to cultural domination has been criticised by writers who challenge the liberal assumptions of the fairness doctrine. They argue that, since cultural domination is often deeply sedimented, it may not be a simple task to challenge dominant norms. In the USA, Richard Delgado and Jean Stefancic argue that it is difficult to challenge the deeply inscribed and routinised

---

[40] See T. Gibbons, *Regulating the Media* (1991), pp. 180–181.
[41] See L. Jaffe, "The Editorial Responsibility of the Broadcaster: Restrictions on Fairness and Access" (1972) 85 *Harv. L.R.* 768.
[42] Gibbons, *op. cit.*, at 180, citing to R. Keat, "Consumer Sovereignty and the Integrity of Practices" in *Enterprise Culture* (R. Keat and N. Abercrombie eds., 1990).

images of black people and minorities which permeate U.S. culture.
While these images change over time, they argue that history shows
that it is extremely difficult to "talk back" to the dominant narrative of
any particular era and that the marketplace of ideas may be valuable
for making incremental changes but not for challenging systemic issues.[43]
A similar style of argument is deployed by Carol Smart in relation to
the difficulties of developing an alternative discourse to the routine
representations of women which "sexualises and limits women".[44]

There are other methods of "talking back" to advertising such as
boycotts, graffiti campaigns and the development of media literacy. But
all attempts to challenge the power of advertising must confront the
increasing dominance of a commercial culture and advertising which
continually associates images of freedom, empowerment and equality
with the private consumption of commodities. This culture raises
fundamental questions about the relationship of markets to democracy.
The central theme of this book is the importance of engaging with the
ground rules of consumer markets: the basic structure within which
advertising operates. There is a need to renew the study of advertising
as a part of competition law. The role of advertising and image
marketing as a form of artificial product differentiation in oligopolistic
consumer markets could be reinvigorated. Trademark law could be
investigated from a critical consumer perspective. The concept of
sustainable consumption should be integrated into economic analyses
of the potentially harmful effects of advertising in industries with
excessive selling costs. Greater attention should be paid to the cultural
damage related to the cumulative effects of advertising images. All of
these initiatives are likely to be controversial since they challenge
powerful corporate interests which increasingly dominate not only
markets for goods but also the market of ideas.

---

[43] See Delgado and Stefancic *op. cit.*
[44] Smart, *Feminism and the Power of Law* (1989), p. 133.

Appendix

Further Reading

The following references include significant texts and articles cited in the text and other writings which may be helpful to those interested in pursuing the themes raised in the book.

Consumer Culture: Consumption and Post-Modernism

The role of consumption and consumerism in contemporary capitalism, its relationship to production, and its significance as a site of social conflict, has been an important theme in recent theoretical writing on Post-Modernism or Post-Fordism. A valuable analysis of these issues may be found in F. Jameson, *Post-Modernism or the Cultural Logic of Late Capitalism* (1991). S. Best and D. Kellner, *Post-Modern Theory: Critical Interrogations* (1991) is a survey of post modern theory. Writers who view consumption as a terrain of struggle include Laclau and Mouffe, and Touraine; see E. Laciau and C. Mouffe, *Hegemony and Socialist Strategy: Towards a Radical Democratic Politics* (1985) and A. Touraine, *The Post-Industrial Society* (1971). B. De Sousa Santos in *Towards a New Common Sense: Law, Science and Politics in the Paradigmatic Transition* (1995) characterizes consumption as "an autonomous structural site of social relations, a new form of power, legality and knowledge" (*ibid.*, at p. 420). The essays in S. Hall and M. Jacques, *New Times: The Changing Face of Politics in the 1990s* (1989) cover such issues as Fordism and Post-Fordism and the Politics of Identity. See also R. Keat, N. Whiteley and N. Abercrombie, *The Authority of the Consumer* (1994). For a critique of Post-Modernism see E. M. Wood, *The Retreat from Class: A New "True"*

Socialism (1986), and see Chapter 7 of T. Eagleton, *Ideology* (1991). For a general discussion of culture and ideology, see J. Thompson, *Ideology and Modern Culture* (1990) and see also the interesting essays by C. Stanley, "Repression and Resistance: Problems of Regulation in Contemporary Urban Culture: Part I: Toward Definition", (1993) 21 *International Journal of Sociology of Law*; Part II "Determining Forces" (1993) 21 *International Journal of the Sociology of law* 121.

There is now a wealth of literature on consumer culture. A recent book which reviews much of this literature and provides many further references is D. Miller (ed.), *Acknowledging Consumption: A Review of New Studies* (1995). There are valuable contributions by, among others, Colin Campbell on the sociology of consumption, David Morley on the debate over active and passive media audiences, and Ben Fine on the limits of neo-classical economics in analysing consumption and consumer choice. See also the introduction to F. Mort, *Cultures of Consumption: Masculinities and Social Space in Late Twentieth Century Britain* (1996) and A. Tomlinson (ed.) *Consumption, Identity, and Style: Marketing, Meanings and the Packaging of Pleasure* (1990). Robert Bocock in *Consumption* (1993) provides a helpful introduction to theories about the nature of consumption and its relation to modern capitalism. See also G. Cross, *Time and Money: The Making of Consumer Culture* (1993). The works of Bordo and Hooks, cited below, are excellent critiques of the culture of consumer capitalism. See also D. Kellner, *Media Culture* (1996) and M. Featherstone, *Consumer Culture and Post-Modernism* (1990). A classic text on the development of consumer culture in the US is E. Barnouw, *Tube of Plenty: The Evolution of American Television* (1975).

Cultural Studies

The development of cultural studies is charted in the introduction to L. Grossberg, C. Nelson and P. Treichler, *Cultural Studies* (1992). There is also useful material on the development of cultural studies in D. Morley and K-H. Chen, *Stuart Hall: Critical Dialogues in Cultural Studies* (1996). See also D. Webster, "The Long Reaction: 'Americanization and Cultural Criticism" in D. Webster, *Looka Yonder! The Imaginary America of Populist Culture* (1988). J. Fiske in *Television Culture* (1987) provides a useful introduction to theoretical influences on the development of cultural studies and discusses some of the studies of "active audiences" by D. Morley, (see, *e.g. Family Television* (1986)) and others. An influential early essay is S. Hall "The Rediscovery of Ideology: Return of the Repressed in Media Studies" in M. Gurevitch, et al., *Culture, Society and the Media* (1982). See also, J. Radway, *Reading the Romance* (1984); D. Hebdige, *Subculture: The Meaning of Style* (1979) and *Hiding in the Light: On Images and Things* (1988); P. Gilroy, *Small Acts* (1993); M. Nava, *Changing Cultures: Feminism, Youth and Consumerism* (1992); F. Mort "The Politics of Consumption" in S. Hall and M. Jacques (ed) *New Times* (1989). P. Bourdieu, *Distinction: A Social Critique of the Judgment of Taste* (Richard Nice, translator, 1986) is important for its analysis of the relationship between culture and class.

On the role of cultural power in sustaining oppression see E. Said, *Orientalism* (1979) and *Culture and Imperialism* (1993). See also J. Pieterse, *White on Black: Images of Africa and Blacks in Western Popular Culture* (1990).

Advertising and Cultural Studies

Some important general texts for those interested in advertising and culture are T. Veblen, *The Theory of the Leisure Class: An Economic Study of Institutions* (1905); B. Friedan, *The Feminine Mystique* (1963); J. K. Galbraith, *The Affluent Society*, (1967); R. Hoggart, *The Uses of Literacy;* R. Barthes, *Mythologies* (1973); R. Williams, "Advertising: the Magic System" in R. Williams, *Problems in Materialism and Culture* (1980). For a direct application to advertising of ideas from cultural studies, see K. Myers, *Understains: The Sense and Seduction of Advertising* (1986). J. Williamson, *Decoding Advertisements: Ideology and Meaning in Advertising* (1978) is a classic analysis of how advertising works. See also B. Bonney and H. Wilson, "Advertising and the Manufacture of Difference" in M. Alvarado and J. O. Thompson (ed), *The Media Reader* (1990). A fascinating analysis of the power of advertising is M. O'Barr, *Culture and the Ad: Exploring Otherness in the World of the Ad* (1994). I also found R. Goldman, *Reading Ads Socially* (1992) of value. Stuart Ewen, *Captains of Consciousness: Advertising and the Social Roots of Consumer Culture* (1976) is an important historical study. Jackson Lears' *Fables of Abundance* (1995) is a rich cultural history of advertising, influenced by the writings of Foucault on disciplinary power and the conception of the "self-regulating subject". A review of Foucault's conceptions of power is found in D. Cooper *Power in Struggle: Feminism, Sexuality and the State* (1995) Chapter 2. An excellent historical source on the ideological role of advertising messages in the USA is Roland Marchand, *Advertising the American Dream: Making Way for Modernity 1920–1940* (1985) and a book which contains many thoughtful reflections on the power of advertising is L. Savan, *The Sponsored Life: Ads, TV and American Culture* (1994). See also M. Schudson, *Advertising, The Uneasy Persuasion: Its Dubious Impact on American Society* (1984); M. Davidson, *The Consumerist Manifesto: Advertising in Post-Modern Times* (1992); J. Berger, *Ways of Seeing* (1973); P. Rutherford, *The New Icons?: The Art of Television Advertising* (1994). There is much of general interest in E. Seiter, *Sold Separately: Parents and Children in Consumer Culture* (1995).

S. Bordo, *Unbearable Weight: Feminism, Western Culture and the Body* (1993) is an excellent feminist critique of the oppressively normalising effects of advertising images of women in consumer capitalism. See also Naomi Wolf, *The Beauty Myth* (1991) and R. Coward, *Female Desires* (1985). The many essays of bell books in, for example, *Yearning; Race Gender and Cultural Politics* (1990), *Black Looks: Race and Representation* (1991) and *Outlaw Culture: Resisting Representations* (1994) present sharp analyses of racism and cultural power.

For further general references on advertising and culture see G. Dyer, *Advertising as Communication* (1988) and W. Leiss, S. Kline and S. Jhally, *Social Communication in Advertising.* (2nd. ed., 1990).

Advertising and the Law

Some of the central articles in the US are R. Brown, "Advertising and the Public Interest: Legal Protection of Trade Symbols" (1948) *Yale L. J.* 1165; Note, "The Regulation of Advertising" (1956) 56 *Colum. L. Rev.* 1018; "Developments in the law—Deceptive Advertising" (1967) 80 *Harv. L. Rev.* 1005. The article by Pitofsky in 1977 had a significant influence in incorporating the idea of advertising as information and conceptualising regulation of advertising as ensuring adequate information for consumers. See R. Pitofsky, "Beyond Nader: Consumer Protection and the Regulation of Advertising" (1977) 90 *Harv L. Rev.* 661. Law and economics scholars have developed this approach. See, for example, H. Beales, R. Craswell and S. Salop, "The Efficient Regulation of Consumer Information" (1981) 24 *Journal of Law and Economics* 491; R. Craswell, "Interpreting Deceptive Advertising" (1985) 65 *Boston Univ. L.Rev.* 657. See also the critique of Craswell by R. Schecter in "The Death of the Gullible Consumer: Towards a More Sensible Definition of Deception at the FTC" (1989) *University of Illinois Law Review* and see reply by Craswell in "Regulating Deceptive Advertising: The Role of Cost-Benefit Analysis" (1991) *Southern California Law Review* 549. An excellent review of theories of advertising regulation in the context of the control of environmental advertising is J. Holder, "Regulating Green Advertising in the Motor Car industry" (1991) *Journal of Law and Society* 323. See also I. Ramsay, "Advertising, Taste Construction, and the Search for Enlightened Policy: A Critique" (1991) 29 *Osgoode Hall L. J.* 573 and "Note-Harnessing Madison Avenue: Advertising and Products Liability Theory" (1994) 107 *Harv. L. Rev.* 895.

A useful review of the different policy objectives for legal regulation of advertising may be found in S. Kline and W. Leiss, "The Ravelled Sleeve: Advertising Policy in Canada" in H. Holmes and D. Taras, *Seeing Ourselves: Media Power and Policy in Canada* (1992). The regulation of lifestyle advertising is discussed in R. Moon, "Lifestyle Advertising and Freedom of Expression" (1991) 36 *McGill L. J.* 76 and a useful article on advertising and product differentiation is E. Mensch and A. Freeman, "Efficiency and Image: Advertising as an Antitrust Issue" (1990) *Duke L. J.* 321. On advertising unfairness see, *e.g.* A. Duggan, "Fairness in Advertising: in Pursuit of the Hidden Persuaders" (1977) 11 *Melbourne L. Rev.* 50; M. G. Jones, "The Cultural and Social Impact of Advertising on American Society" (1970) 8 *Osgoode Hall L. J.* 65; "Note-Fairness and Unfairness in Television Product Advertising" (1978) 76 *Mich. L. Rev.* 498.

The development of the doctrine of commercial speech in the US and Canada has stimulated theoretical work on the relationship between advertising, consumer culture and democracy. Some contributions to this debate include O. Fiss, "Free Speech and Social Structure" (1986) 71 *Iowa L. Rev.* 1405; R. Coase, "Advertising and Free Speech" in Hyman and Johnson (ed), *Advertising and Free Speech* (1977); C. Sunstein, "Free Speech Now" (1992) 59 *University of Chicago Legal Forum* 255; F. Schauer, "The Political Incidence of the Free Speech Doctrine" (1993) 64 *Univ. of Colorado L. Rev.* 635; K. Sullivan, Free Speech and Unfree Markets" (1995) 42 U.C.L.A. L. Rev. 949; T. Jackson and J. Jefferies,

"Commercial speech: Economic Due Process and the First Amendment" (1979) 65 *Virginia L. Rev.* 1; A. Hutchinson, "Money Talk: Against Constitutionalizing (Commercial) Speech" (1991) 17 *Canadian Business Law Journal* 2; R. Sharpe, "Commercial Expression and the Charter" (1987) 37 *University of Toronto L. J.* 229. See also R. Collins and D. Skover, *The Death of Discourse* (1996), and symposium in 1993 *Texas Law Review*; H. Schiller, *Culture Inc.* Chapter 3; G. Edwin Baker, *Advertising and a Democratic Press* (1994).

For comparative analyses of the role of advertising law see D. J. Harland, "The Legal Concept of Unfairness and the Economic and Social environment: Fair trade, Market law and the Consumer Interest" in E. Balate (ed.) *Unfair Advertising and Comparative Advertising"* (1988). This book also contains essays which outline the German approach to advertising regulation which includes it within the general framework of regulation of unfair competition. For an early analysis of this approach see W. Grimes, "Control of Advertising in the United States and Germany: Volkswagen has a Better Idea" (1971) 84 *Harv. L. Rev.* 1769. See also Bob Schmitz, "Advertising and Commercial Communications Towards a Coherent and Effective EC Policy" (1993) 16 *Journal of Consumer Policy* 387. For an international analysis of advertising see A. Mattelart (translated by M. Chanan) *Advertising International: The Privatisation of Public Space* (1989) and there is discussion of advertising in S. MacBride, *Many Voices, One World: Communication and Society, Today and Tomorrow* (UNESCO: 1980) and see J. Sinclair, *Images Incorporated: Advertising as Industry and Ideology* (1987) at Chapters 5–7.

The role of advertising images as unfair cultural practices is one aspect of larger explorations of the role of cultural images in sustaining oppression. See Bordo above and C. MacKinnon, *Only Words* (1993). See R. Delgado and Jean Stefancic, "Minority Men, Misery, and the Marketplace of Ideas" in M. Berger, B. Wallis and S. Watson (eds) *Constructing Masculinity* (1995) at 211. The article by K. Crenshaw, "Race, Reform and Retrenchment: Transformation and Legitimation in Anti-Discrimination Law" (1988) 101 *Harv. L. Rev.* 1331 is valuable and see also M. Matsuda, et al., *Words that wound: critical race theory, assaultive speech and the First Amendment* (1993). A useful overview of different feminist approaches to the role of media images in sustaining oppression is L. Van Zoonen, *Feminist Media Studies* (1994).

Index

163